ENDORSEMENTS FOR:
What the Bible Says: Oils and Spices Revealed

"If you want to learn about biblically based medicine and how to heal naturally, then I recommend reading What the Bible Says: Oils and Spices Revealed. This book provides a clear, biblical understanding of the origins of oils and spices, while challenging the reader with biblical truths that are relevant today. Erica McNeal combines faith, history, science, and personal experiences that will deepen our understanding of essential oils, while bringing us closer to the One who created them."

—Dr. Josh Axe DC, CNS, Founder of www.DrAxe.com

"What the Bible Says is a must read for any Christian venturing into the world of understanding how powerful God's natural medicine is and how it aids in our physical, emotional, and spiritual healing. This book gives voice to the rich tradition of essential oils in the Bible. Erica paints beautiful scriptural scenes of how oils were used in ancient days, and how we can in turn use them in our modern day lives. She threads together biblical references, science, and experience to give us a new pathway to devotion and balance."

—Mary Crimmins, Personal Life Coach & Business Coach
www.marycrimmins.com

"Erica does an amazing job of helping us understand the history of essential oils and how they were used during biblical times. You will be blown away by how intelligent and loving our Creator is in that He gave us these plants in nature to help our bodies heal. What the Bible Says is broken down into easy-to-read sections, with excellent references and thought-provoking truths straight out of the Bible. This is a book everyone needs to have in their resource arsenal."

—Kristen Pardue, Registered Dietician
www.NaturallyFreeRD.com

"What the Bible Says is a great resource for digging into the history and uses of oils in biblical times. It is also a beautiful modern-day story of Erica McNeal's journey and how these oils have changed her life. This book carries a deep message of hope that is as old as the oils themselves, yet just as powerful."

—Traci Scheer, Business Mentor and Coach
www.intentionallybalanced.com

"Erica does an amazing job of bringing the oils of the Bible alive. Not only does she share her knowledge of oils, but also shares her personal experiences and walk with God in a way that spoke volumes to my heart. This book is not only educational, but a great tool to help deepen your relationship with God. I highly recommend What the Bible Says: Oils and Spices Revealed to anyone who wants a deeper understanding of the essential oils mentioned in the Bible and a deeper relationship with the Author."

—Cristina Johnson, Health and Wellness Advocate

"What a great resource for understanding the use of essential oils and their ties to ancient Bible times and traditions! Erica McNeal's approach is so clear and so readable. I loved delving into the Bible a bit deeper and learning about the individual uses for the twelve oils. Will recommend to all my friends and colleagues!"

—Dr. Renée N. Hale, Owner and Lead Consultant
WellSpirit Consulting Group, Inc.
www.wellspiritconsulting.com

"History, Scripture, faith, and health all come together in this study of essential oils and spices. Culture of biblical times is described with great clarity in how the oils and spices were used, and sheds a fresh perspective on modern day life. What the Bible Says is a perfect addition to the library of anyone looking to deepen their knowledge of essential oils."

—Cheryl Valleroy, Health and Wellness Advocate

"What the Bible Says: Oils and Spices Revealed not only gives us a beautiful historical review on how oils and spices were used in the Bible, but offers a poignant perspective on suffering and the love of God. I loved every page, and highly recommend it to anyone who is interested in adding to their knowledge of oils and spices. As a nurse practitioner who received my education from a highly respected main-stream medical university, but who now frequently turns to natural medicine and essential oils for answers to troubling medical questions and preventive therapies, I found this book to be not only very educational, but an encouragement and inspiration."
—Melissa Braun, RN, MSN, Health and Wellness Advocate

"What the Bible Says is an easy read, as Erica McNeal intermingles her personal story with facts and faith. It is a beautiful picture of the history of essential oils as a gift from our Creator! Erica shares her in-depth knowledge and years of studies with us, wrapping it all in and around personal experience, making it very relevant and meaningful. Embracing the mystery of our amazing God, while demystifying the gift of essential oils.

As a Registered Nurse who has spent many years with modern medicine, I am encouraged to see works such as this book remove the 'magic' from essential oils and reveal the practical, yet amazing healing properties that have been in use for centuries by those who have not relied on reductionist interpretation of science. This is a must read for anyone interested in being empowered to go beyond what modern science currently allows and explore all of our options for life as our Creator intended."
—Juli Reynolds, RN, www.reimaginingwellness.com

What the Bible Says

What the Bible Says

Oils and Spices Revealed

ERICA MCNEAL

This book is dedicated to my incredible team of oilers.
Each and every day you inspire and encourage me.

As a former essential oil critic, I was humbled to discover that the very branch I hung my criticism on contained the brilliance of God to bring balance and healing to my body.

Erica McNeal

Table of Contents

Section One

A Biblical Foundation

Chapter One

Should Christians Use Essential Oils?

"Then God said, 'Let the earth sprout vegetation, plants yielding seed, and fruit trees on the earth bearing fruit after their kind with seed in them';
and it was so. The earth brought forth vegetation, plants yielding seed after their kind, and trees bearing fruit with seed in them, after their kind;
and God saw that it was good."

Genesis 1:11-12

I used to be in the camp where I thought essential oils were weird. I only knew a few people who used oils, and each person had a more holistic and natural approach to health care than I did. Honestly, I didn't understand why people would rub oil on their bodies, use herbs to treat illness, or eat dirt as probiotics, instead of popping a pill or turning to modern medicine. With my medical history of cancer and child loss, I'd built up a lifetime of trusting in modern medicine for every ache and pain, and on more than one occasion, my very life.

To further the discomfort I felt for essential oils, I found that my brain automatically translated the word "aromatherapy" to "New Age" and "crystals". My ignorance made me uncomfortable because I listened to the loudest voice: the one that talked about finding your "chi", or your "energy", or your "life force"—none of which I knew were lost or why I should be looking for them in the first place! So, I disregarded the voices of well-intentioned people who were trying to offer help in ways I was seeking, but who didn't provide the answers I thought I was looking for.

Then everything changed!

We were at Disney World and our three-year-old son was having the mother of all meltdowns *before* we even got into the park. Now, I get Disney World is overwhelming and can be very over-stimulating. But friends, we were standing in the *entrance line* just trying to get *into* the magical kingdom when our son began to scream hysterically over ants—ants that were five feet away from him! I have no clue how he even saw them, and could certainly not understand why they bothered him so much.

Had we not been meeting friends in the park, I would have turned around and gone home. It was *that* bad. Ten minutes later when we reached our friends I was DONE, totally and completely wiped out from his hysterics!

Seeing what was happening, my friend Traci asked if she could try something on him. In total and complete exasperation, I said, "Girl, I don't care what you give him. If you can make this stop, make it stop!"

Traci placed an essential oil blend meant to bring focus and calming on the back of our son's neck. Within minutes our out-of-control boy was totally chill, calm, and collected, bending down playing with the ants on the ground. Did you catch that? *He was playing with the ants!*

Had I not seen this meltdown recovery unfold with my own eyes, or had other witnesses to remind me I was not dreaming, I would not have believed it. And, this wasn't just a momentary blip in his freak-out session; our son stayed relaxed and calm throughout the rest of the day and all through the night. At that point I was hooked. I told Traci I would need "that stuff" (whatever it was) by the gallons.

In that moment I decided it was finally time to pull back the curtain of essential oils and take a deeper look. What I found completely rocked my world as I began to uncover hundreds of references to plants, spices, and oils used in the BIBLE. While I'd read the Bible cover to cover more than once, somehow I'd totally missed this!

As a recovering Essential Oil Critic, I have come a long way from my original understanding of what essential oils are, what they are not, and how they should be used. If you are anything like me, perhaps you have also struggled with wondering if using essential oils are compatible with a faith in God. I know the debate is out there, so let me share with you three reasons why Christians can in good, clear conscious use essential oils.

1. The problem is NOT with using essential oils, but in having an unclear understanding of where oils come from.

Modern-day essential oils (and even the infused oils of the Bible which we will uncover soon) all come from the vegetation God created.

> "Then God said, 'Let the earth sprout vegetation, plants yield-ing seed, and fruit trees on the earth bearing fruit after their kind with seed in them'; and it was so. The earth brought forth vegetation, plants yielding seed after their kind, and trees bearing fruit with seed in them, after their kind; and God saw that it was good." *Genesis 1:11-12*

In His infinite wisdom, God created plants and trees to be our source of food and to sustain our life.

> "Then God said, 'Behold, I have given you every plant yielding seed that is on the surface of all the earth, and every tree which has fruit yielding seed; it shall be food for you; and to every beast of the earth and to every bird of the sky and to every thing that moves on the earth which has life, I have given every green plant for food'; and it was so. God saw all that He had made, and behold, it was very good. And there was evening and there was morning, the sixth day." *Genesis 1:29-31*

One could even argue that a plant-based diet might be everything our human bodies need for optimum health and wellness; for a plant-based diet is exactly what God provided as nutrition for Adam and Eve. It wasn't until ten generations later (roughly 1,100 years), in the time of Noah (after the flood), that God gave animals to become another source of food to sustain our bodies. Up to that point, all nutrition came from seed-bearing plants.

> "Every moving thing that is alive shall be food for you; I give all to you, as I gave the green plant." *Genesis 9:3*

2. The problem is NOT with using oils, but in how the use of oils has been distorted.

Since the beginning of time, most of what God has created has found a way to become distorted. Look at sex, marriage, food, relationships; even some of the angels – who were in the very presence of God – found a way to become corrupt. The problem is not with the essential oils themselves, but the way humans have once again distorted something God called "good."

Because many people in the New Age movement encourage people to use essential oils in ungodly ways, it is easy to perceive essential oils as "bad." And yet, essential oils are the very immune system of plants, protecting the plant from disease and bringing healing when needed. Think about how the very creativity and wisdom of God allows for plants and humans to have a similar structure—creating a unique relationship where plants have the ability to help our human bodies heal themselves.[1]

3. The problem is NOT with using oils, but in how the oils have become branded.

Most of my initial exposures to essential oils were hearing of them being used for "spiritual awakenings" and in ways that are meant for God alone to spiritually uncover. I would hear of people using oils to "guard against negative energy", to "enhance spirituality", or to try and bring about visions and dreams of the future. Therefore, I branded essential oils as being "scary" and "bad", because of the appearance that they were being used as a form of spiritual manipulation. However, like many things in life, I don't believe this was God's original intention!

If we want to re-brand what has become corrupted in the eyes of many people, we must first educate ourselves with a clear, biblical understanding of where oils come from, how they were used in biblical times, and how we can use them appropriately today. We must also be gentle in the way we respond to the concerns of others, and careful in how we market these products. Essential oils are not meant to replace God; they are not "miracle drugs", nor are they the answer to every medical problem we face. In fact, if I fall down and break my leg, please don't rub an oil on me; take me to the doctor!

While essential oils can aid our bodies, God created our bodies to be *MIRACULOUS!*

Imagine what would happen if our skin never healed itself. We'd walk around with open cuts and wounds oozing blood everywhere we went. (That's a pretty gross picture, isn't it?) Now think about how our bodies constantly create blood, produce different tears based on why we are crying,[2] fight bacteria and viruses, and constantly pump blood through our veins. This happens every second of every day. Again, miraculous!

Unfortunately, despite our best efforts, sometimes we still get sick! In those times, I am so incredibly grateful that essential oils are a God-given, natural way to help our bodies heal. And, as I keep my eyes on the Maker and Creator of not only these plants, but more importantly, my very soul, I find confidence and peace in His wisdom and design to give us this incredible resource. In my journey to find health and wellness, I have learned that I am able to honor God when I choose alternative therapy for my family because essential oils are simply another way He has chosen to provide for us.

Chapter Two

Just Keep Surfing

"By the river on its bank, on one side and on the other, will grow all kinds of trees for food. Their leaves will not wither and their fruit will not fail. They will bear every month because their water flows from the sanctuary, and their fruit will be for food and their leaves for healing."

Ezekiel 47:12

Ezekiel 47:12 is the Jeremiah 29:11 of aromatherapy. Both verses are often taken literally, and well out of context, when there is so much hidden beneath the surface.[3] Many people will use the passage in Ezekiel to show biblical "proof" that modern day essential oils are meant to provide healing to our bodies. While plants are absolutely a gift from God, and the very makeup of their leaves, stems, seeds, roots, bark, and flowers are able to help our bodies heal themselves, this is where most people stop with this Bible verse.

Let's not do that! Let's dig deep friends—because this verse is about so much more than oils. And, I really think as we unveil the true meaning and intent behind this verse, it will ROCK your world!

Before we are able to understand the context of this verse, we must look at the context of the book of Ezekiel found in the Old Testament. This book is written by the prophet himself, contains seven different God-given visions, and can be broken down into the following three sections:

1. The judgment on Israel (chapters 1–24).
2. The judgment on the nations (chapters 25–32).
3. The future blessings and prophecies of hope and salvation for Israel (chapters 33–48).

To place Ezekiel 47:12 into its proper context, we must have an understanding of the prophet's final vision found in Ezekiel 47:1-12.[4] This vision is about grace, love, hope of salvation, and redemption—all rolled into one.

In this text Ezekiel is being led into a flowing river. This symbolism is highly significant of a person's relationship with God and the different depths of relationship a believer will encounter as he or she matures in his or her faith.

This relationship begins when a person steps into the water and is *ankle-deep* (47:3). When someone becomes a believer, he or she is making a decision to accept that Jesus Christ is God's Son, that although sinless, He died on a cross and He rose again to be the ultimate sacrifice needed to pay the price for our sins and restore our relationship with God.

As this person reads and obeys the Bible, he or she is led into a deeper relationship with God where the water comes to his or her *knees* (47:4). Some biblical scholars believe the intention of the word *knees* in this verse refers to a believer's prayer life; for a person is unable to grow in his or her relationship with God without spending time with Him in prayer.[5]

As this person continues to grow in his or her relationship with God, he or she walks into waters to his or her "loins", or waist (47:4). The water now forces the person to think through his or her actions, inactions, and decisions, as the water now has a greater impact on the way a person is able to move.

And finally, when this person decides that he or she is all in, he or she will *swim* (47:5). The believer has now reached the place where he or she must exercise complete faith. Swimming requires constant movement to avoid being swept away by the current in the water and to prevent the body from sinking. This is especially necessary when a person is in water over his or her head or the waves begin to come their way.

When I was growing up, I loved to surf!

Even now, if you put me on a beach that desire to hop on a surfboard will instantly well up within me. I learned early on in surfing that no matter how hard I tried to avoid the big waves, they always came. While I was able to go around some waves and over others, often times I needed to use a *duck dive* to go through the wave.

A duck dive is a surfing maneuver where lying down on my board, I would put my head down and straighten my arms, forcing my surfboard to sink into the water. I would then shove the back of the board down with my foot to keep the board steady and go through the center of the wave. The board was just an extension of my body and we moved as one.

The same is true of our relationship with God. There are some trials we will be able to go around, and perhaps some we skim the surface of. We may even think we can handle the smaller ones on our own.

Other trials however, are so big that we are required to make a decision. Will we try to take on that giant wave on our own, only to end up with a mouth full of salty water and sand-filled shorts after being tossed about the ocean? Or, will we put our head down in prayer, take a deep breath, and be so connected to God that relying on His power to help us overcome our circumstances becomes our first response?

This was never truer for me than when, at twenty-two years old, I was diagnosed with a rare type of cancer that had only previously been found in men over the age of eighty. In a single breath I came face to face with what I believed about God, and had to make a decision of whether I was going to continue *swimming* and keep my complete faith in Him, or if I was going to stop moving and allow myself to be swept away by all the raging currents of fear and anxiety.

It has been fifteen years now since I first had cancer. In the years since, I have gone through two more cancer relapses and my husband and I have also experienced extensive and devastating child loss. Our eleven-year old marriage has endured a great deal of trauma and pain. But, the greatest lesson we have learned through the onslaught of big waves is that it is impossible to exercise our faith if we stop moving. While there is definitely a time to be still and rest, we rest as an act of faith, not as one who gives up hope.

The very definition of *exercise* tells us that this is an activity requiring physical or mental effort. The same goes for our faith relationship. When we exercise our complete faith in God, even in the Big Kahuna of all waves, we choose to keep surfing. And, when we come out on the other side of the wave that was intended to destroy us, we find that we never had to face the wave alone and we went deeper in our relationship with Jesus than we ever thought we could go!

Chapter Three

Our Rock and Healer

*"By the river on its bank, on one side and on the other, will grow all kinds of
trees for food. Their leaves will not wither and their fruit will not fail.
They will bear every month because their water flows from the sanctuary, and
their fruit will be for food and their leaves for healing."*

Ezekiel 47:12

Friends, are you ready to dive deep? In this chapter we will uncover the
incredible richness of Ezekiel 47:12 by breaking this verse down one section
at time.

By the river on its bank, on one side and on the other,
will grow all kinds of trees for food.

The *trees* referred to in this verse are the true believers in Jesus Christ.
Just as trees have roots, believers are rooted in the love of God, in the person of Christ, and in the Holy Spirit. And because of this, we are designed to
bring forth *food*.

> "I am the vine, you are the branches; he who abides in Me and
> I in him, he bears much fruit, for apart from Me you can do
> nothing." *John 15:5*

In Scripture, believers are compared to the most steadfast trees such as palm trees, cedars, olives, and myrtles.

> "The righteous man will flourish like the palm tree, he will grow like a cedar in Lebanon." *Psalm 92:12*

> "So they will be called oaks of righteousness, the planting of the LORD, that He may be glorified." *Isaiah 61:3b*

Their leaves will not wither

In many places around the world, you will find a true season of autumn, when the trees, which were once vibrant and fruit bearing, begin to change colors and die. In the same way, there are many believers who, as they go through the difficulties of life, walk away from their relationships with God. Over time, their spiritual lives begin to fade and die as well.

However, believers who continue to trust in God regardless of their circumstances remain grafted in God so that their roots, branches, seeds, leaves, flowers, fruit, and sap—every part of their very existence—remains bound to the source of strength only He is able to provide.

> "For he will be like a tree planted by the water, that extends its roots by a stream and will not fear when the heat comes; but its leaves will be green, and it will not be anxious in a year of drought nor cease to yield fruit." *Jeremiah 17:8*

Think of a time when you have gone through something difficult. Did anyone ever tell you, "God will not give you more than you can handle?" Can I please apologize on their behalf? Because this is totally and completely wrong! The first time I had cancer, this phrase was said to me so many times, that I got my Bible out and tried to look it up. I looked and looked and looked, and guess what? It's not in the Bible!

I believe this common Christian cliché comes from an inaccurate interpretation of 1 Corinthians 10:13, which states:

"No temptation has overtaken you but such as is common
to man; and God is faithful, who will not allow you to be
tempted beyond what you are able, but with the temptation
will provide the way of escape also, so that you will be able to
endure it."

The writer of Corinthians, Paul, is addressing sin issues, not common
trials or tribulations for the people of Corinth. He is warning them to avoid
the temptation to repeat the sinful acts that were found in Israel's (at that
time) recent history. He is asking these people to stay away from idolatry,
sexual immorality, and the desire to test God. The reality friends is that God
will allow us to be stretched beyond our human capabilities in order to show
us our need for Him, to deepen our faith, and to show us that His strength
is limitless.[6]

But, there is HOPE!

We were not created to handle our circumstances alone. If as a *tree*,
we remain steadfast in our relationship with God, He becomes our source
of strength regardless if we are in a time of peace or braving a Category 5
hurricane.

and their fruit will not fail.

This portion of Ezekiel 47:12 is referring to the future works of the Holy
Spirit. When a person chooses to place his or her faith in Jesus Christ, he or
she will be filled with the Holy Spirit (our Counselor and Guide).

"Peter said to them, 'Repent, and each of you be baptized in
the name of Jesus Christ for the forgiveness of your sins; and
you will receive the gift of the Holy Spirit.'" *Acts 2:38*

As the Holy Spirit works in us, our lives begin to change and we learn
how to bear the fruit of the Spirit as described in Galatians 5:22-23 "love, joy,
peace, patience, kindness, goodness, faithfulness, gentleness and self-control."

These *fruits* will never fail or die, as the impact of the work of the Holy Spirit in and through our lives has an eternal impact, and is evidence of a person's faith in Jesus Christ.

They will bear every month

The Hebraic word used for *bear* here is *bâkar*, which translated means *first fruits*. This means that every month (every single day), a believer (the *tree*) needs to not only remain in God, as we can do nothing apart from Him, but to produce *fruit* by acting on his or her faith. Remember, these *works* do not earn us salvation, but come from the gratitude of the price Jesus paid for our salvation.

Here are 10 suggestions of how we can show our love for God any day of the week:

1. Make a meal for someone in need.
2. Visit someone in the hospital.
3. Offer free childcare to parents or caregivers for a night out.
4. Bring a care basket to a grieving family.
5. Pray for the person who just cut you off in traffic, instead of reacting in anger.
6. Go out of your way to do a random act of kindness for someone you have a difficult relationship with.
7. When someone asks for prayer, pray with or for him or her on the spot.
8. Leave a generous tip for your waiter or waitress and write a note saying, "Jesus Loves You!"
9. Be authentic and real with others.
10. Buy a meal for the person behind you in the drive-thru.

Friends, there is no retirement in our relationship with Jesus. Every month, every single day, we are to exercise our faith in Jesus Christ and share our love of God with others.

"They will still yield fruit in old age; they shall be full of sap and very green, to declare that the LORD is upright; He is my rock, and there is no unrighteousness in Him." *Psalm 92:14-15*

because their water flows from the sanctuary,

It is not by our own abilities that we grow in our relationship with Jesus Christ and *bear fruit*, but through the grace of God (the sanctuary) and the Gospel. As we allow God to work in and through us, we are able to grow in our faith, to love others, and to *bear fruit*.

In order for a tree to live, let alone produce fruit, it must be continually nourished by water; otherwise the tree will wither and die. In the same way, when a believer chooses not to be fed and nourished by God, his or her spiritual life and relationship with God will wither and potentially die. To remain nourished, a believer needs to read his or her Bible, talk to God in prayer, spend time with other believers, and go to church on a consistent basis.

and their fruit will be for food

This food is not for the believer, as a believer's nourishment comes from God, but rather this food is for other people. A believer produces food when he or she acts on his or her faith in God in tangible ways. For instance: evangelism, helping the poor, caring for orphans, serving his or her community, teaching, serving and loving others, and using personal experiences to build relationships.

"The fruit of the righteous is a tree of life, and he who is wise wins souls." *Proverbs 11:30*

While it is fairly easy to find "good Christian things" to do to produce food and show our love for God, it is much more difficult to live out our faith when we are personally under fire. Though people can see and follow our example of serving at a homeless shelter or raising money for a charitable cause; people will watch us more closely when difficulties hit to see how we respond in our circumstances.

This does not mean that our family and friends are looking for us to have all the right answers or to behave perfectly in all situations. In fact, I think it is more detrimental to the cause of Christ when Christians act like everything is perfectly okay when circumstances should suggest otherwise. People need to see that Christians are real and authentic, that we hurt and have emotions that are sometimes ugly, dark, and difficult to understand. The difference in our times of trouble is that we do not hurt as one without hope.

The key to producing eternal food is to not just act on the brokenness around us, but to also share the HOPE we have in Jesus Christ when the brokenness happens TO us.

When we become the bereaved, the broken, the diagnosed patient, the one burying a child, or the one whose life has been turned upside down, are we going to become (or remain) bitter and angry?

Will we drown in our desperate desire to find the purpose or reason why this happened to *us*?

Or, could we work through our brokenness relying on God, one step (sometimes one hour) at a time to eventually find a purpose in the emotional scars and pain that linger?

Imagine how much food Christians could produce if we all took our personal brokenness to help and love others. This world would be a different place! For, when we become the broken, we are given a unique understanding and insight into the emotions others face. Because of this, when we share our painful experiences we have the ability to care more deeply and can help people to not feel alone in their circumstances. Fifteen years ago, I was hit hard with this unexpected reality.

"Nineteen-year-olds are not *supposed* to have CANCER."

This thought consumed my mind the entire week I spent at a Bible Camp. I was tired; exhausted from a long summer traveling as a representative for my college. I didn't understand why I was in Oregon that week, as the camp really did not seem to need me. Then I met this boy named Shay.

I'd played volleyball with him for three days when he suddenly collapsed on the ground in exhaustion. I had no idea his body was fighting a disease. Through light-hearted vulnerability he shared his story about having an advanced form of cancer. What started out as a small lump grew significantly in a very short amount of time. He'd already been through multiple surgeries and too many tests to keep track of.

He should have been throwing caution to the wind and chasing his wildest dreams. Instead, he was about to begin his first round of chemotherapy. His faith was firm, no hint of fear or anger, yet he was still real and authentic about the journey it took for him to get to that point. He knew he belonged to Jesus and appeared to genuinely accept his circumstances. I listened to his story stunned, trying not to touch the hard lump that had been developing underneath my jawbone all summer long.

Looking at him you'd never know he was sick. His smile, happiness, and love for God permeated his entire being. His faith inspired me as he lived out 1 Timothy 4:12:

"Let no one look down on your youthfulness, but rather in speech, conduct, love, faith and purity, show yourself an example of those who believe."

He breathed this example into every person who learned of his story. The last night of camp I wondered if I could ever face something like cancer and stand firm in my faith. Honestly, I did not know the answer!

Just three short weeks later I walked out of the doctor's office attempting to grasp the fact that I too had cancer. Even as those words were spoken, I resolved to take the example I had seen in Shay and made the conscious choice to keep my total faith and confidence in God, regardless of the outcome.

I never spoke to or saw Shay again after that last day of camp. I don't even know if he is alive today, and if he is, whether or not he would remember me.

But because he lived out his faith during his battle with cancer, he gave me an example of how to be real and authentic when my own battle with cancer showed up. He strengthened my faith and prepared me for my cancer journey before I even knew I would need it. But, God knew!

And, here's the beauty... the *food* that has been produced by Shay's example to me was never tangible for him. He never saw it, or even knew it existed. However, the impact of his faith led to a life-long harvest in my life, and continues with every person who is touched by our ministry.

Friends, you may never know when your faith and authenticity can lead someone into a deeper relationship with God. So, let's stop simply checking the good little Christian boxes or pretending that life is perfect and start *living out our faith*! You never know whom you are equipping for the unexpected!

and their leaves for healing.

Uncovering this last section of Ezekiel 47:12 overwhelmed me in such an awe-inspiring way. The Hebraic word used for healing here is *terûphâh* which literally means "healing" or "medicine" and is only used one time in the entire Bible—right here in this verse!

The root words for terûphâh come from two Hebraic words:
1. rûph = rock
2. râphâ' = healer and physician – most often used as a name of God.

Discovering this gem rocked my world, (no pun intended) because in the New Testament, Jesus is personally referred to as the "rock":

> "For I do not want you to be unaware, brethren, that our fathers were all under the cloud and all passed through the sea; and all were baptized into Moses in the cloud and in the sea; and all ate the same spiritual food; and all drank the same spiritual drink, for they were drinking from a spiritual rock which followed them; and the rock was Christ."
> *1 Corinthians 10:1-4*

Let's not forget about all the numerous verses that refer to God the Father as the ROCK in the Old Testament.

> "There is no one holy like the LORD, indeed, there is no one besides You, nor is there any rock like our God." *1 Samuel 2:2*

> "On God my salvation and my glory rest; the rock of my strength, my refuge is in God." *Psalm 62:7*

When you put all of these verses together, they reveal the beautiful and direct relationship between God the Father and His Son, Jesus Christ. In the book of Ezekiel, God is revealing that true healing can only come through Jesus Christ (rock) as the ultimate Healer (rapha).

Isn't that incredible?

While I was studying this Bible verse, our church was in the middle of a 21 Days of Prayer event. These three weeks were great and challenged me in many ways. Thousands of people met every morning at the church or online to pray for each other, for our country, for our family, friends, and personal lives. As I prayed through different prayer requests, one theme continually surfaced—the need for healing: physically, financially, and relationally. And, one Bible verse continually came to my mind over these situations:

> "No weapon that is formed against you will prosper."
> *Isaiah 54:17a*

What about the weapon of illness?
Of desperation?
Of divorce?
Of child loss?
Of bankruptcy?

NO, not ONE shall prosper!

This doesn't mean God will heal all of our illnesses this side of Heaven, or instantly restore all of our relationships, or take away our child loss. It means that when we choose to trust in the name of Jesus Christ—regardless of the outcome—our circumstances do not need to have power over us.

Yes, this side of Heaven we will still grieve and we will still hurt, but we can still choose the way we respond to our circumstances. And, we can find hope that through the death and resurrection of Jesus Christ, we have access to an eternal healing that NO weapon can ever destroy with God as our Rock and Healer.

Chapter Four

Infused Oils Vs. Steam Distillation

*"But He was pierced through for our transgressions, He was crushed
for our iniquities; the chastening for our well-being fell upon Him,
and by His scourging we are healed."*

Isaiah 53:5

Essential oils as we know them today were not used in biblical times. In fact, the current popular method of extracting oils by steam distillation was likely centuries away from being used when Jesus walked this Earth. Healing oils of the biblical age were infused oils, made largely from softening, mashing, pressing, crushing, grinding, or soaking plant matter in olive oil, palm oil, or fat.[7]

To infuse something simply means to transfer the scent, flavor, and healing or therapeutic properties of one object to another. In medical science, we see a variety of infusion processes, including medicine given through an IV, blood transfusions, intramuscular injections, epidurals, or even skin and bone grafts. We can also see infused products every time we walk down the aisles of our grocery stores. Next time you go shopping, check out all the flavored cooking oils, vinegars, herbal teas, coffees, and all those yummy flavored chocolate bars.

While today we have plenty of ways to crush and grind our own material, in the book of Numbers we are given a glimpse into how plant material was crushed in biblical times when God gave the Israelites manna.

> "The people would go about and gather (the manna) and grind it between two millstones or beat it in the mortar, and boil it in the pot and make cakes with it; and its taste was as the taste of cakes baked with oil." *Numbers 11:8*

What is interesting to me is that according to Exodus 11:5, slave women were normally the ones using the hand mills and mortar to crush the wheat, barley, grain, and in this case, the manna. The hand-mill consisted of two stones, the upper stone being movable and slightly concave, while the lower stone being stationary. According to the Holman Dictionary, two women facing each other worked the mill. One woman would feed the grain, while the other woman would guide the crushed product into little piles.

The grain would then feed into the central hole of the upper stone and gradually work itself down between the stones. As the grain reduced to flour, it would fly out from between the stones onto a cloth or skin placed underneath the mill. To make fine flour, the flour would then be reground and sifted once again.[8] As you can imagine, the task of grinding and crushing plant material was a very laborious job, but also one that was considered the lowest employment in the house or given to someone as a form of punishment and condemnation. As a side note, this makes me think of Jesus!

> "But He was pierced through for our transgressions, He was crushed for our iniquities; the chastening for our well-being fell upon Him, and by His scourging we are healed." *Isaiah 53:5*

In this verse, the Prophet Isaiah is prophesying the death of Jesus Christ who would be condemned to die for our sins in order to bring healing to the world. Though sinless, Jesus willingly took on this punishment so that our relationship with God could be restored.

"And He Himself bore our sins in His body on the cross, so that we might die to sin and live to righteousness; for by His wounds you were healed." *1 Peter 2:24*

I love how the Bible constantly interweaves the beautiful story of God's love for us. And, here's what is fascinating: when the material to be crushed changed from wheat or barley to specific plants, spices, and olive oil, the responsibility of making perfume and anointing oils became one of honor, and held high esteem for the best perfumer in the trade.

"Then the LORD said to Moses, 'Take for yourself spices, stacte and onycha and galbanum, spices with pure frankincense; there shall be an equal part of each. With it you shall make incense, a perfume, the work of a perfumer, salted, pure, and holy.'" *Exodus 30:34-35*

It is important for us to understand that the infused oils used in biblical times were very different and less concentrated than the essential oils we use today. That being said, the Bible does provide many examples where even these less potent, infused oils were used for amazing purposes.

Steam Distillation

Since the oils in the Bible were infused oils, I'd like to share with you the process of extracting essential oils from steam distillation, so we can better understand the differences between the two. Of note, some essential oils (mostly fruit) are cold-pressed distilled. However, the majority of modern day essential oils are steam distilled.

During the process of extracting essential oils through low-heat steam distillation, steam passes through the plant material. With a combination of the steam and just the right amount of pressure, the essential oils are released.

As the oils are released, the vapor mixture flows through a condenser, cools down, and the water and oils naturally separate, leaving two layers. The essential oil rises to the top and is separated from the water, much like a bottle of Italian dressing separates when not being used. This allows the oil to be collected in its purest form.[9]

While there are many people who still practice the art of infused oils, the potency in essential oils is so much greater and has a much longer shelf life! Just one drop of essential oil contains approximately 40 million-trillion molecules. This number is mind-blowing when you understand that our bodies only have 100 trillion cells. Therefore, ONE drop of essential oil contains enough molecules to cover every cell in our bodies with 40,000 molecules. So, you can see why even a small amount of pure essential oil can have profound effects on the body, our brain, and our emotions.[10]

Chapter Five

Old Testament Oil

"There is precious treasure and oil in the dwelling of the wise,
but a foolish man swallows it up."

Proverbs 21:20

The Old Testament was originally written in Hebrew, a beautiful language designed to give the reader a picture of meaning. Therefore, one biblical Hebrew word is not simply defined by one or two other words, rather a paragraph of imagery, as if trying to place the reader back into the biblical setting where the events once unfolded.

The Hebrew language only has about six thousand words, derived from about five hundred roots. This is why one word can have such a wide variety of meanings, sometimes making it difficult to understand the intention of the author. This is also one reason why we have so many different translations of the Bible.

The more I study Hebrew and Greek (the original languages of the Bible) the more I am amazed at how remarkable their ability is to have multiple levels of understanding and truth. How many times have you found encouragement in the Bible, only to later realize that a verse is either not at all what you thought it was about, or the had such a deeper, more meaningful impact on your life? This happens to me often; and while at times I am

27

truly humbled and need to eat my words, other times I am totally blown away by how the love of God comes out in ways I never anticipated.

In order to uncover the true purpose of the Author, sometimes we need to take a deeper look at the historical context, syntax, and utilize the amazing resources from biblical scholars who have spent their lives studying the Bible. When I find myself struggling to understand a Bible verse or concept, I often turn to the Interlinear, along with Biblical Concordances, Dictionaries, and Encyclopedias found on StudyLight.Org.

Shemen

"There is precious treasure and oil in the dwelling of the wise, but a foolish man swallows it up." *Proverbs 21:20*

In the King James Version (KJV) and New American Standard Version (NASV) the word *olive* is omitted in front of the word *oil* in Proverbs 21:20. This has led some people, especially those who market aromatherapy, to believe this verse is referring to infused oils, much like we previously discussed. However to understand this verse in context, this is one of those instances where we must take a deeper look to gain an accurate understanding of intent.

The Hebrew word for oil used here in Proverbs is *shemen*, used 193 times in the Old Testament. Simply translated, *shemen* means fat, olive oil, oil, or ointment and is derived from the root word *shaman*, meaning to be or to become fat.[11]

By the definitions above, we are able to deduce that Proverbs 21:20 is not referring to infused oils, which do not contain fatty lipids or acids, and therefore make them very different from vegetable or animal fats. In context, the word *shemen* here refers to olive oil, which had four different uses in the Bible:

1. Food
2. Ointment
3. To illuminate a lamp
4. Soap

Olive oil was a staple in biblical times because it was so incredibly useful. As Matthew 25:1-13 reminds us, those who were wise used all of their resources, in this case olive oil, well.

In the Old Testament, when the Bible refers to healing oils (what we use today as essential oils) the oils were either called by name (myrrh, frankincense, cassia, etc.), or there was an additional noun in front of the word *shemen*.

The Hebrew noun *tôb*, means "precious" and when used in front of *shemen* signifies expensive or valuable infused oils.

> "Hezekiah listened to them, and showed them all his treasure house, the silver and the gold and the spices and the precious (tôb) oil (shemen) and the house of his armor and all that was found in his treasuries. There was nothing in his house nor in all his dominion that Hezekiah did not show them."
> *2 Kings 20:13*

Taking this a step further, when nouns *mishchâh* or *moshchâh* are used in front of the word *shemen*, this is signifying a holy or anointing oil.

> "Take also for yourself the finest of spices: of flowing myrrh five hundred shekels, and of fragrant cinnamon half as much, two hundred and fifty, and of fragrant cane two hundred and fifty, and of cassia five hundred, according to the shekel of the sanctuary, and of olive oil a hin. 'You shall make of these a holy anointing (mishchâh) oil (shemen), a perfume mixture, the work of a perfumer; it shall be a holy anointing (mishchâh) oil (shemen).'" *Exodus 30:23-25*

Chapter Six

Giving Jesus Your Best

"Teacher, which is the great commandment in the Law?" And He said to him, 'You shall love the Lord your God with all your heart, and with all your soul, and with all your mind.' This is the great and foremost commandment. The second is like it, 'You shall love your neighbor as yourself.' On these two commandments depend the whole Law and the Prophets."

Matthew 22:36-40

I remember my very first day of Introduction to Greek. My college professor stood at the front of the room with a slightly smug look on his face. Once he gained everyone's attention, he said, "There are three things you should know about this class. 1) I wrote the book you are using to learn Greek. 2) In the Greek language, there are twenty-four different ways to say the word "the". And 3) I do not sign withdrawal papers to allow anyone to drop my class." As my jaw dropped to the desk, I took in a deep breath and knew I was in for a very long semester.

The Greek language is not only fun to learn how to write, but is another language where one English word cannot even come close to capturing the depth or meaning of the original intent. For example, there are three different Greek words in the Bible that translate into the English word "love". Yet, the meanings of these three Greek words have different depths depending on which word is being used.

Agape is an unconditional love; whereas *phileo* is a brotherly love, and *storge* is the kind of love and affection that happen between a husband and a wife.

The importance of understanding the different meanings become clear when you look at the Greek text of John 21:15-17. You will see the different words *agape* and *phileo* being used in the conversation between Jesus and Peter. Unfortunately, the significance of this verse is missed in most English translations.

After His death, burial, and resurrection, Jesus reinstated Peter back into ministry after Peter denied Jesus before the crucifixion. Here is the conversation between these two recorded in the Gospel of John.

> "Jesus said to Simon Peter, 'Simon, son of John, do you love (agape) Me more than these?' He said to Him, 'Yes, Lord; You know that I love (phileo) You.' He said to him, 'Tend My lambs.'
>
> He said to him again a second time 'Simon, son of John, do you love (agape) Me?' He said to Him, 'Yes, Lord; You know that I love (phileo) You.' He said to him, 'Shepherd My sheep.'
>
> He said to him the third time 'Simon, son of John, do you love (phileo) Me?' Peter was grieved because He said to him the third time, 'Do you love (phileo) Me?' And he said to Him, 'Lord, You know all things You know that I love (phileo) You.' Jesus said to him, 'Tend My sheep.'"

Did you notice how Jesus asked Peter twice if he unconditionally loved (agape) Jesus, with Peter responding that He loved Jesus with the word meant for brotherly love (phileo)? Let that sink in for a few moments.

murou

In the New Testament, the word for anointing oil is *murou*. While there are thirty-four variations of this Greek word, this word is only used fourteen times in the Bible and means perfume or fragrant oil. According to the

Brown-Driver-Brigg's Lexicon on Study Light, *murou* is derived from these two Greek words:

1. *môr* = myrrh, an Arabian gum from the bark of a tree, used in sacred oil and in perfume
2. *miphrâś* = to spread out

We see an incredible use of *murou* in the Gospel of Mark 14:3-9:

> "While He (Jesus) was in Bethany at the home of Simon the leper, and reclining at the table, there came a woman with an alabaster vial of very costly perfume (murou) of pure nard; and she broke the vial and poured it over His head. But some were indignantly remarking to one another, 'Why has this perfume (murou) been wasted? For this perfume (murou) might have been sold for over three hundred denarii, and the money given to the poor.' And they were scolding her.
>
> But Jesus said, 'Let her alone; why do you bother her? She has done a good deed to Me. For you always have the poor with you, and whenever you wish you can do good to them; but you do not always have Me. She has done what she could; she has anointed My body beforehand for the burial. Truly I say to you, wherever the gospel is preached in the whole world, what this woman has done will also be spoken of in memory of her.'"

This amazing act of love is one of the few stories recorded in all four Gospels. You will also find it in Matthew 26:7, Luke 7:37-38, and John 12:3, with Mark recording that the oil poured over the head of Jesus was a "very expensive perfume, made of pure nard." By pouring this oil over Jesus, she anointed His body for His imminent burial (Mark 14:8).

Many biblical scholars agree that this anointing oil was Spikenard: "pure nard, un-mixed and genuine; or liquid nard, which was drinkable, and easy to be poured out."[12]

In his Commentary of the Bible, Matthew Henry points out that it was a custom for people who were condemned to die to have their coffins prepared and other provisions made for their funerals while they were still alive.[13] This woman not only prepared the body of Jesus Christ for his death and burial, but this was also the very first time anyone acknowledged His fate, even though Jesus had spoken openly that He was to die.

What is also beautiful about this verse is that this woman "broke the jar", meaning she gave the very best of *every last drop* she had to Jesus. Now, here's the reality check for me: how often do I do this; give Jesus the best of *everything* I have? (Ouch!)

We sure seem to check the boxes, don't we?

Did you read your Bible? (Check the box.)
Pray at mealtime? (Check the box.)
Go to church? (Check the box.)

It is so easy for the Christian life to become mundane and routine. We allow ourselves to become so busy with the demands and joys of life that rarely do we stop to give Jesus our very *best*, let alone our *good*.

However, our relationship with God should not be stale and boring! When we live each day actively seeking ways to love God and love others, our relationship with God (and others) becomes more alive and exciting! When we look at *everything* we have: our time, money, resources, house, spouse and children as being on loan from God, we tend to appreciate the value even more.

Not only is our Creator so incredibly deserving of our love, adoration, and distraction-free time, but the deeper we dive into the Word of God, the more we stay focused on Him. The more we choose to dive deeper into a relationship with Him, the more our lives transform in love, grace, and the ability to relate to others.

Friends, it is time for us to stop responding to God in *phileo*, when He asks us if we *agape* Him!

Section Two

A Study of 12 Oils
and Spices in the Bible

Chapter Seven

Aloes/Sandalwood

*"Nicodemus, who had first come to Him by night, also came, bringing
a mixture of myrrh and aloes, about a hundred pounds weight."*

John 19:39

Biblical aloes/sandalwood were extracted from the dark, non-function-
ing central core of the evergreen tree. While this part of the tree no longer
uses water, it functions as the primary way to support the tree. Aloes/san-
dalwood has a sweet, woody, and fruity scent, and while it can be confused
with the ever-popular aloe vera plant, they are completely different.

Hebrew word: 'ăhâlîym = aloe tree or perfume

How many references are there to 'ăhâlîym in the Old Testament? Four

- Numbers 24:6
- Psalm 45:8
- Proverbs 7:17
- Song of Solomon 4:14

Greek word: alóē = aloe

How many references are there to alóē in the NT? One

The only time the word *aloes* is referenced in the New Testament is in John 19:39-40 when *aloes* was used to prepare the body of Jesus Christ for burial.

> "Nicodemus, who had first come to Him by night, also came, bringing a mixture of myrrh and aloes, about a hundred pounds weight. So they took the body of Jesus and bound it in linen wrappings with the spices, as is the burial custom of the Jews."

Biblical and Historical Uses: Religious ceremonies, perfume (Psalm 45:8, Proverbs 7:17) and embalming (John 19:39)

Modern Day Uses: Acne, Asthma, Bronchitis, Candida, Colds and Flu, Cough, Dermatitis, Skin Disorders, Stress, Throat Infections, Yeast Infections

Plant Properties: Antibacterial, Anti-depressant, Anti-fungal, Anti-inflammatory, Antiseptic, Aphrodisiac, Carminative, Disinfectant, Diuretic, Expectorant, Sedative, Stimulant

Modern Day Fun Fact: Modern day aloes/sandalwood is steam distilled from the wood of small tropical evergreen trees in the genus *Santalum* found in locations such as Hawaii and India.

Did you know that aloes/sandalwood have a 90% sesquiterpene level, a compound molecule only found in plants and insects?[14] According to Dr. David Hill, sesquiterpenes molecules:

1. Deliver oxygen molecules to cells, like hemoglobin does in the blood.

2. Can erase or deprogram miswritten codes in the DNA.

3. Are thought to be effective in fighting cancer because the root problem with a cancer cell is that the cells contain misinformation; and these molecules can erase that miswritten information. Also, the oxygen carried by sesquiterpenes can create an environment where cancer cells cannot reproduce. Therefore, these molecules not only disable cancer's coded misbehavior, but can also stop its growth.[15]

In his research on the blood brain barrier, Dr. David Stewart reports:

"The American Medical Association (AMA) has said that if they could find an agent that would pass the blood-brain barrier, they would be able to find cures for ailments such as Lou Gehrig's disease, multiple sclerosis, Alzheimer's disease, and Parkinson's disease. Such agents already exist and have been available since Biblical times. The agents, of course, are essential oils — particularly those containing the brain oxygenating molecules of sesquiterpenes."[16]

Biblical History: The custom of the Jews to prepare a body for burial was done with great reverence and care. Immediately following the death of a Jew, the body would be washed (Acts 9:37) and wrapped in linen cloths layered with spices and ointments (John 19:39-40). The face was also covered with a special type of face cloth (John 20:7).

While this was taking place in some cities, orders would be given to hire mourners to wail and lament over the dead. We see this especially in Matthew 9:23 when a synagogue official came to Jesus to ask him to heal his daughter who had just died. By the time Jesus arrived at the official's home, a noisy crowd of mourners had already gathered.

To transport the body to the grave, the body was laid in an open bed coffin, sometimes known as a burial couch[17] and was taken outside city limits (Luke 7:12-14). The women, hired mourners, relatives and friends led the way to the final resting place of the dead. The crowd gathered in this fashion, and given the noise of those wailing, this part of the burial process must have been obvious and would have garnered a lot of attention.[18]

In contrast, Joseph of Arimathea (a man considered to be a disciple of Jesus, though not one of the twelve) quietly sought Pilate to prepare and wrap the body of Jesus for burial. At this same time, Nicodemus, a Pharisee and member of the Sanhedrin, also came to the body of Jesus to anoint His body with myrrh and aloes.

While these two men followed the Jewish customs of preparing the body of Christ for burial, there is no mention of large crowds or people being paid to mourn. Nor is there mention of a large procession honoring the body of Jesus to the location of his grave. Matthew 27:61 simply tells us that Mary Magdalene and "the other Mary" were sitting nearby when Joseph and Nicodemus laid the body of Jesus to rest.

How painful for God the Father to watch these events unfold. Of all people who deserved the loudest noise and wails, it would have been Jesus. But, the people at that time did not see Him for who He was. I know God is all knowing and knew this response and rejection was coming. But, as a mama who has also buried a child, I can't help but consider the hurt God must have felt watching so few people even acknowledge the death of His Son.

Chapter Eight

Cassia

*"All your garments are fragrant with myrrh
and aloes and cassia."*

Psalm 45:8a

Biblical cassia was peeled from the inner bark of an East Asian tree called *Cinnamomum cassia*. Likely imported from India, cassia is in the same family as cinnamon. The Hebrew root word for cassia is *qâtsaʻ* and indicates the need for someone to scrape or cut off the bark from the tree.

Hebrew word: There are two different words used in the biblical Hebrew language for cassia:

1. qiddâh = spice or cassia
2. qetsiy'âh = derived from the Greek *kasia* and refers to the strips of bark used to extract the oil

How many references are there to qiddâh and qetsiy'âh in the Old Testament?

qiddâh is used twice:
- Exodus 30:24
- Ezekiel 27:19

qetsiy'âh is used once:

• Psalm 45:8

Greek word: kasia = cassia

How many references are there to kasia in the NT? None

Biblical and Historical Uses: Cassia was part of the sacred and holy anointing oil given to Moses by God for anointing purposes (Exodus 30:24-25) and was also used as perfume.

Modern Day Uses: Arthritic Pain, Colds and Flu, Constipation, Cough, Diarrhea, Stomach Ache

Plant Properties: Antibiotic, Anti-diarrhea, Antiseptic, Anti-spasmodic, Antiviral, Astringent, Disinfectant, Stimulant

Modern Day Fun Fact: Modern day cassia essential oil is steam distilled from the *Cinnamomum cassia* tree and has a warm, spicy scent. If you have cinnamon spice in your home, you likely have cassia—as this form of cinnamon is the most commonly used and sold cinnamon in the United States. True cinnamon, or *Cinnamomum zeylanicum*, is lighter in color and sweeter.

In a study done by the Pennington Center, researchers found cassia cinnamon greatly "improve(d) blood glucose, triglyceride, total cholesterol, HDL cholesterol, and LDL cholesterol levels in individuals with type 2 diabetes."[19]

Biblical History: Cassia was one of the ingredients in the Holy Anointing Oil given to Moses.

> "Moreover the LORD spake unto Moses, saying, 'Take thou also unto thee principal spices, of pure myrrh five hundred shekels, and of sweet cinnamon half so much, even two hundred and fifty shekels, and of sweet calamus two hundred

and fifty shekels, and of cassia five hundred shekels, after the shekel of the sanctuary, and of oil olive an hin: and thou shalt make it an oil of holy ointment, **an ointment compound after the art of the apothecary**: it shall be a holy anointing oil.'" *Exodus 30:22-25 (KJV)*

I found the King James Version of this Bible verse fascinating, as the KJV is known to be one of the closest word for word translations of the Bible from its original languages. In these verses we find the very first time the word *apothecary* is used in the Bible, often translated in other versions as *perfumer*. What's interesting here is the use of the two Hebrew words, *mirqachath* and *râqach* in this verse.

> "An ointment compound (mirqachath) after the art of apothecary (râqach)..."

Mirqachath comes from the primitive root word *râqach* meaning to mix a compound of spice and oils. Once again this is where the English language sometimes falls short of expressing the richness of the Hebraic text. To me, a perfumer is someone who would make something that smells lovely, whereas someone who is in the art of apothecary is a person who creates medicine or compounds meant to bring healing to the body. As we find in Exodus 30:26-28,30 this sacred oil anointed:

> "...the tent of meeting, the ark of the testimony, the table and all its utensils, the lampstand and its utensils, the altar of incense, the altar of burnt offering and all its utensils, the laver and its stand... Aaron and his sons that they may minister as priests to (God)."

We see in the Bible that different people prepared the ointments, based on the ointments' purposes. However, only those appointed by God could prepare the Holy Anointing Oil. In Exodus 31:1-11 we find that after filling them with wisdom and discernment, God appointed Bezaleel and Oholiab to prepare the sacred ointment and the incense used for the holy place in worship. The priestly families were also responsible for the production of the large amount of ointments necessary for Temple use according to 1 Chronicles 9:30.

According to the Holman Bible Dictionary, those who prepared the Holy Anointing Oil were "to take the many gums, resins, roots, and barks and combine them with oil to make the various anointments used for anointing purposes. In many cases, the formula for these ointments and perfumes was a professional secret, handed down from generation to generation."[20]

Chapter Nine

Cedar/Cedarwood

"He (King Solomon) also spoke 3000 proverbs, and his songs were 1,005. He spoke of trees, from the cedar that is in Lebanon, even to the hyssop that grows on the wall; he spoke also of animals and birds and creeping things and fish. Men came from all peoples to hear the wisdom of Solomon, from all the kings of the earth who had heard of his wisdom."

I Kings 4:32-34

Biblical cedarwood was extracted from the bark and core of the cedar trees found in Lebanon.

Hebrew word: 'erez = cedar or cedar wood

How many references are there to 'erez in the Old Testament? Sixty-Nine

- Leviticus 14:4, 14:6, 14:49, 14:51, 14:52
- Numbers 19:6, 24:6
- Judges 9:15
- 2 Samuel 5:11, 7:2, 7:7
- 1 Kings 4:33, 5:6, 5:8, 5:10, 6:9, 6:10, 6:15, 6:16, 6:18, 6:20, 6:36, 7:2, 7:3, 7:7, 7:11, 7:12, 9:11, 10:27

- 2 Kings 14:9, 19:23
- 1 Chronicles 14:1, 17:1, 17:6, 22:4
- 2 Chronicles 1:15, 2:3, 2:8, 9:27, 25:18
- Ezra 3:7
- Job 40:17
- Psalm 29:5, 80:10, 92:12, 104:16, 148:9
- Song of Solomon 1:17, 5:15, 8:9
- Isaiah 2:13, 9:10, 14:8, 37:24, 41:19, 44:14
- Jeremiah 22:7, 22:14, 22:15, 22:23
- Ezekiel 17:3, 17:22, 17:23, 27:5, 31:3, 31:8
- Amos 2:9
- Zechariah 11:1, 11:2

Greek word: kédros = cedar

How many references are there to kédros in the NT? None

Historical Uses: Purification rites, building material for royal buildings (1 Kings 5:6-10, 9:11; 2 Chronicles 2:16; Ezra 3:7), signified power and wealth, growth and strength

Modern Day Uses: Acne, Alopecia, Anxiety, Dandruff, Eczema, Psoriasis and other skin disorders, Skin care, Wounds

Plant Properties: Analgesic, Astringent, Calming, Insect Repellant, Sedative

Modern Day Fun Fact: Alopecia is a type of hair loss that occurs when the immune system attacks hair follicles. In many cases the result is total and complete hair loss. Cedarwood has proven itself to be one of the oils that can help stimulate hair growth in patients with alopecia and re-grow hair.

In a study found in the National Center for Biotechnology Information (NCBI), researchers conducted a randomized trial of eighty-six patients.

Forty-three patients were given a mixture of thyme, rosemary, lavender, and cedarwood mixed with a carrier oil (often a vegetable oil used to dilute essential oils before being placed on the skin) to massage on their scalp every day. The other forty-three patients were only given a carrier oil to massage into their scalp.

Forty-four percent of the patients who received the essential oils saw significant improvement, while only 15% of the control group saw some improvement. The conclusion was that treatment for alopecia with essential oils was significantly more effective than treating with the carrier oil alone.[21]

Biblical History: In biblical times the cedar tree of Lebanon was known for its glory (Isaiah 35:2), strength (Psalm 29:5), height (2 Kings 19:23), long branches (Ezekiel 31:3-9), durability (1 Kings 6:9-10) and majesty (Zechariah 11:1-2).

The cedar was one of the most valuable trees used as building material for boards, pillars, ceilings, and to make carvings of wood (1 Kings 10:27, Jeremiah 22:14, Isaiah 44:14-15).

Cedar is also mentioned twice for ritual cleansing. In Leviticus 14:4 after being cleansed, the leper was to sprinkle a mixture of the blood of a clean bird, cedar wood, scarlet, and hyssop. Also, in Numbers 19:6 cedar wood, hyssop, and scarlet were used during the cleansing ritual after coming in contact with a dead body.

In some Bible verses, "cedars of Lebanon" are referenced to, causing some confusion with actual cedar wood. Biblical scholars believe the "cedars of Lebanon" may be a different type of tree than the "cedar wood", even though both use the same Hebrew word erez. It is believed the Cedars of Lebanon were more specifically *Cedrus Libani*, while the "cedar wood" was more likely *Juniperis phoenicea* or *Juniperus Sabina*, both found in the wilderness.[22] All three trees are in the same Kingdom (*Plantae*), Division (*Pinophyta*), Class (*Pinopsida*) and Order (*Pinales*), however in a different Family, Genus and Species.

Chapter Ten

Cypress

*"The glory of Lebanon will come to you, the juniper, the box tree and
the cypress together, to beautify My sanctuary; and I shall make
the place of My feet glorious."*

Isaiah 60:13

Biblical cypress was extracted from the branches and leaves of the
evergreen cypress tree, a native of Taurus. The most ancient living cypress
is located in Abarkooh, near Shiraz and is estimated to be approximately
4,000 years old. Today, cypress essential oil is often extracted from cypress
trees in Southern Europe.

Hebrew word: There are four different Hebrew words for cypress.

1. berôsh = cypress
2. berôth = cypress, fir, juniper, pine
3. te'ashshûr = a species of tree (perhaps cypress)
4. tirzâh = a type of tree (perhaps cypress)

How many references are there to berôsh, berôth, te'ashshûr, tirzâh in
the Old Testament?

berôsh is used twenty times:

- 2 Samuel 6:5
- 1 Kings 5:8, 5:10, 6:15, 6:34, 9:11
- 2 Kings 19:23
- 2 Chronicles 2:8, 3:5
- Psalm 104:17
- Isaiah 14:8, 37:24, 41:19, 55:13, 60:13
- Ezekiel 27:5, 31:8
- Hosea 14:8
- Nahum 2:3
- Zechariah 11:2

berôth is used once:

- Song of Solomon 1:17

te'ashshûr is used twice:

- Isaiah 41:9, 60:13

tirzâh is used once:

- Isaiah 44:14

Greek word: kyparíssi = cypress

How many references are there to kyparíssi in the NT? None

Historical Uses: Purification and Ship Building

Modern Day Uses: Arthritic Pain, Asthma, Colds and Flu, Diarrhea, Excess Perspiration, Hemorrhoids, Menopause, Menstrual Problems, Muscle Pain, Sore Throat, Stress, Varicose Veins

Plant Properties: Antibacterial, Antibiotic, Antiseptic, Anti-spasmodic, Astringent, Diuretic, Disinfectant, Sedative

Modern Day Fun Fact: Did you know your lymphatic system is unable to drain itself, but rather relies on your body's movement in order to circulate and drain properly? This is why lymphatic massage and rebounding exercises are so effective. These two actions squeeze your lymph nodes to get all the junk out. Who knew those huge trampolines in the backyard served a greater purpose than keeping children occupied for an hour.

In a similar way, cypress essential oil can aid our lymphatic system by promoting circulation and is one of the most recommended oils for heart disease, aneurisms, neuropathy, poor circulation, rheumatoid arthritis, pleurisy, and preeclampsia.

Biblical History: In Genesis 6:14 we read:

> "Make for yourself an ark of *gopher* wood; you shall make the
> ark with rooms, and shall cover it inside and out with pitch."

When God told Noah to build the ark out of gopher wood, Noah knew exactly what God was referring to. We do not, not exactly. Gopher wood is only used once in the entire Bible, right here in the book of Genesis. While the exact tree is unknown, some people believe the ark was made of pine or cedar. However, the popular understanding from biblical scholars is that the ark was actually made of cypress wood.[23]

The term *gopher wood* has no Hebrew root, which has led many to believe it to be a general name for a tree, instead of an actual gopher tree, which to our knowledge does not exist. Cypress however, was known in the Bible to be used to build ships, as we find in Ezekiel 27:5, and many modern translations of the Bible use the word cypress in lieu of gopher wood in Genesis 6:14 (for instance, NIV and NLT).

Chapter Eleven

Frankincense

"After coming into the house they saw the Child with Mary His mother; and they fell to the ground and worshiped him. Then, opening their treasures, they presented to Him gifts of gold, frankincense and myrrh."

Matthew 2:11

Biblical frankincense came from the resin of the *Boswellia* tree, which was imported from Arabia (Isaiah 60:6 and Jeremiah 6:20), and also grew in Palestine.[24] When the resin from the *Boswellia* trees was burned it created a fragrant odor.

Hebrew word: lebônâh = a yellow or white resin burned as fragrant incense

How many references are there to lebônâh in the Old Testament? Twenty-One

- Exodus 30:34
- Leviticus 2:1, 2:2, 2:15, 2:16, 5:11, 6:15, 24:7
- Numbers 5:15
- 1 Chronicles 9:29

- Nehemiah 13:5, 13:9
- Song of Solomon 3:6, 4:6, 4:14
- Isaiah 43:23, 60:6, 66:3
- Jeremiah 6:20, 17:26, 41:5

Greek word: libanos = frankincense

How many references are there to libanos in the NT? Two

- Matthew 2:11
- Revelation 18:13

Historical Uses: Frankincense was one of the gifts of the Magi given to Jesus after his birth. It was used as an ingredient in the Holy Incense (Exodus 30:34), with grain offerings (Leviticus 2:1, 15, 16, 6:15), with memorial offerings (Leviticus 24:7) as a perfume (Song of Solomon 3:6), and for incense (Isaiah 43:23, 60:6, 66:3, Jeremiah 6:20).

Modern Day Uses: Asthma, Bronchitis, Cuts and Wounds, Dermatitis, Indigestion, Neurological Disorders, Scarring, Skin Disorders, Sore Throat, Stomach Ache, Tumor Reduction

Plant Properties: Analgesic, Antidepressant, Anti-fungal, Anti-inflammatory, Antiseptic, Astringent, Cellular protection, Diuretic, Expectorant, Sedative

Modern Day Fun Fact: According to Dr. David Hill, 95% of cancers are not genetic, but rather are a result from damaged DNA because of free radicals, toxicity, and poor nutrition.

As you may know, there is coding in our bodies that inform our cells to know when it is time for the cells to die off. In cancer cells, the process of cell death is blocked and therefore these cancer cells become very difficult to eliminate. This is why such high doses of chemotherapy and radiation are given to patients with cancer—to force apoptosis (cell death).

The problem with chemotherapy and radiation is that in most cases, these treatments are unable to decipher between the healthy cells and the damaged cells, tissues, or organs, thus damaging everything in their path and creating massive side effects.

One of the most remarkable attributes of frankincense is that this essential oil can actually get inside the cell to either repair damaged cells, or, if the cell is unable to be repaired, frankincense can stimulate apoptosis.[25]

Personally, I've already had radiation therapy twice, and chemotherapy once. Unfortunately, my doctors have repeatedly told me that my cancer *will* continue to return until medical science can catch up to my cancer to find out what is causing it to occur. And, even worse, I am running out of modern-day medical solutions to treat my type of cancer.

I am unable to have any more radiation to my head and neck (where my cancer was found all three times), and I had an anaphylactic reaction to the most effective chemotherapy known for my type of cancer. In fact, the chemo almost killed me!

Just days after my chemotherapy infusion, the doctors believed I was having a pulmonary embolism, heart attack, and/or stroke. After a lot of testing, the doctors found out that I am highly allergic to mice antibodies, which were found in this particular chemotherapy. This allergic reaction caused significant side effects for me, including inflammation around my heart (pericarditis), chest pain and pressure, asthma, and trouble breathing that lasted for three years. The majority of these side effects did not stop until I began to incorporate essential oils into my daily regimen.

Therefore, the medical research on frankincense essential oil gives me hope—that what was once given to my sweet Jesus may some day help reduce or even eliminate a recurrence of cancer in my body.

Biblical History: When the Magi came to worship Jesus Christ, they brought three gifts: gold, frankincense, and myrrh. The gift of gold was a gift of providence for the family of Jesus, but could also have been significant of the Magi paying tribute to Jesus Christ as their King.

"Where is He who has been born King of the Jews? For we saw His star in the east and have come to worship Him." *Matthew 2:2*

The gift of frankincense was a gift of experience. Known in the Bible to be a symbol of the divinity of God (Song of Solomon 1:3, Malachi 1:11), when Frankincense is burned the aroma is both fragrant and pleasing. Having the wisdom and discernment that can only come from God, this gift of the Magi could have symbolized their recognition of the divinity of Jesus Christ.

"They said to him, 'In Bethlehem of Judea; for this is what has been written by the prophet: 'And you, Bethlehem, land of Judah, are by no means least among the leaders of Judah; for out of you shall come forth a ruler who will shepherd My people Israel.'" *Matthew 2:5-6*

The gift of myrrh would have been a highly unusual gift to give to a child, as it was primarily used in the Bible for embalming the dead. However, this gift could have symbolized the Magi's recognition that Jesus would fulfill the prophesy of Isaiah and ultimately die to provide salvation to those who would call upon His name.

"For He grew up before Him like a tender shoot, and like a root out of parched ground; He has no stately form or majesty that we should look upon Him, nor appearance that we should be attracted to Him. He was despised and forsaken of men, a man of sorrows and acquainted with grief; and like one from whom men hide their face He was despised, and we did not esteem Him. Surely our griefs He Himself bore, and our sorrows He carried; yet we ourselves esteemed Him stricken, smitten of God, and afflicted. But He was pierced through for our transgressions, He was crushed for our iniquities; the chastening for our well-being fell upon Him, and by His scourging we are healed." *Isaiah 53:2-5*

Our Three Gifts

Quite a few years ago my husband and I started a Christmas tradition in our family. Instead of unleashing a torrent of toys on our children, we choose three gifts to give to our kids (in addition to their stockings) on Christmas morning.

Following the example set forth by the Magi, we give our children a gift of value (gold), a gift of experience (frankincense), and a gift of practicality (myrrh). As parents, we desire to not only set a tone of gratitude in our children, but to continually point our kids back to God, who gave us the most incredible gift of salvation through Jesus Christ.

The gift of value might be a toy or item the kids really want or have been asking for. The monetary value doesn't need to be high, but we look more at the item's value through the eyes of our child. Last year, this meant Lego® sets for our son whose eyes would go wide any time he saw those tiny middle-of-the-night torture devices. For our daughter, this valuable gift was a children's educational tablet where she could play games, draw, read, take pictures and create her own videos.

The gift of experience is something we can do together as a family. Sometimes this is a gift we can use all year long; other times this gift is a one-time event. Over the last few years, we have chosen experiences such as a family trip, local Zoo or Science Center annual passes, or creating a gift that encompasses all the ideas our kids come up with of, "Mom, can we go..."

This past year, we individually wrapped up gift cards to create twelve family fun nights, one to be used for each month of 2015. We have gift cards to be silly and goofy, as well as gift cards to look out for the needs of others. Our purpose with this gift of experience is to create life-long memories with our children by spending quality time together and sharing God's love.

Half of our family fun nights will be focused on our family, while the other half will be focused on loving others. When it is time for our family fun night to begin, we will randomly unwrap one of the envelopes and go off on our adventures. There is little planning to do, because the work has already been done.

Inside each envelope there is either a gift card or cash with the following themes:

1. Purchase indoor snowball fight items. We want the kids to get creative, think outside the box, and most of all have fun with this.

2. Secretly pay for someone else's meal at a restaurant.

3. Purchase some kind of make-at-home kit. This might be ice cream, s'mores, a gingerbread house, whatever we see that sparks an interest that night.

4. Buy food and supplies to bring to a local food pantry or church.

5. Purchase items for Crazy Dinner. Each person chooses what he or she wants to eat for dinner that night and we have a potluck.

6. Secretly tape $1 bills on random items at a discount or dollar store.

7. Family movie night. This is not something we do regularly, so our hope is that this will be a special treat for the kids.

8. Put together care packages and make thank you cards for deployed military members.

9. Buy a small gift for another family member.

10. Purchase ingredients to bake cookies and deliver our sweet treats to our neighbors.

11. Check out a new restaurant.

12. Purchase baby items to bring to a local pregnancy center.

The gift of practicality may seem boring to most, and perhaps may need to become more exciting as our children get older. But for now, we have chosen to give something our children are in need of. This may be a winter jacket, pajamas or a bathrobe, a new outfit, a piece of furniture for their rooms, or new comforter/sheet set for their beds.

Celebrating Christmas this way enables our family to *enjoy* the Christmas season instead of dreading the weeks of self-induced chaos and stress. Our gifts are simple, but well thought out and meaningful!

Christmas celebrates the birth of Jesus Christ. This is a day of celebration and joy that we don't want to rush through or miss because we are consumed by sales, crowds, and the commercialism of Christmas. Instead, we have more time to build gingerbread houses, and decorate cookies, and watch over-the-top sappy romantic Christmas movies, and spend valuable time together every night. The pressure is off and our days leading up to Christmas are relaxed, allowing us to enjoy and soak up the season for what it truly means, instead of what it has become.

Chapter Twelve

Galbanum

"Then the LORD said to Moses, 'Take for yourself spices, stacte and onycha and galbanum, spices with pure frankincense; there shall be an equal part of each. With it you shall make incense, a perfume, the work of a perfumer, salted, pure, and holy. You shall beat some of it very fine, and put part of it before the testimony in the tent of meeting where I will meet with you; it shall be most holy to you.'"

Exodus 30:34-36

Galbanum is believed to come from the branches of the *Ferula galbanifula*, a plant that grew in Syria.

"This gum comes in pale-colored, semi-transparent, soft, tenacious masses, of different shades from white to brown. It is rather resinous than gummy, and has a strong unpleasant smell, with a bitterish warm taste. When distilled with water or spirit, it yields an essential oil, and by distillation in a retort without mixture, it yields an empyreumatic oil of a fine blue color, but this is changed in the air to a purple."[26]

Hebrew word: chelbenâh = resin or gum

How many references are there to chelbenâh in the Old Testament? One

- Exodus 30:34

Greek word: liváni = resin or gum

How many references are there liváni in the NT? None

Historical Uses: Holy Incense (Exodus 30:34)

Modern Day Uses: Cold and Cough, Decongestant, Digestive, Intestinal Problems, Spasms, Wounds

Plant Properties: Analgesic, Anti-Arthritic, Antibacterial, Anti-Parasitic, Anti-Rheumatic, Anti-Spasmodic

Modern Day Fun Fact: Galbanum is composed of 66% resin and 6% volatile oil. The Greeks and Egyptians used galbanum as a stimulant and anti-spasmodic medicine. Today, galbanum is still used on some indolent tumors.[27] Of note, the galbanum resin can be found in the entire plant, not just in the roots, as is the case for many other plants.[28]

Biblical History: Of all the resins and the spice used in the Holy Incense, we know the least about galbanum. As I studied Exodus 30:34, I uncovered two interesting facts.

1. Galbanum was not believed to be a beautiful scent, but rather an unpleasant and bitter scent. Therefore scholars believe galbanum was likely included in the Holy Incense as a base resin, which would allow the Holy Incense to retain its fragrance longer.[29]

2. The Holy Incense found here in Exodus 30:34 is different than the Holy Anointing Oil that we uncovered from Exodus 30:23. The ingredients of the Holy Incense were stacte, onycha, galbanum, and frankincense.

The Hebrew root for *stacte* means to distill, leading some scholars to believe *stacte* was really distilled myrrh.[30] As we will uncover in a few chapters, *onycha* also had an unpleasant odor, which leaves one curious as to why God used both galbanum and onycha to make the Holy Incense.

I can only come to the conclusion that when mixed together, the individual scents combined to create a beautiful and pleasing aroma to our Creator; for this incense was not to be used for personal use, but was set apart as holy for God alone and used to anoint the tent of meeting, or tabernacle.

I love how Matthew Henry, a theologian ordained in England, brings the Holy Incense found in the Old Testament back to Jesus in his Commentary of the Bible.

> "This (Holy Incense) was prepared once a year—the Jews say—a pound for each day of the year, and three pounds over for the day of atonement. When it was used, it was to be beaten very small: thus it pleased the Lord to bruise the Redeemer when he offered himself for a sacrifice of a sweet-smelling savour."[31]

Chapter Thirteen

Hyssop

"You shall take a bunch of hyssop and dip it in the blood which is in the basin, and apply some of the blood that is in the basin to the lintel and the two door-posts; and none of you shall go outside the door of his house until morning."

Exodus 12:22

Belonging to the mint family, hyssop is believed to be an indigenous plant local to western Asia. There are many different theories as to the exact species of hyssop used in the Bible. Some scholars believe this plant was a species of *Marjoram origanum*. Other scholars believe it was the caper plant, the *Capparis spinosa*. And still others believe it is the common bush-like shrub *hyssop*.[32] The oil would have been extracted from the stems and leaves.

Hebrew word: 'êzôb = hyssop, a plant used for medicinal and religious purposes

How many references are there to 'êzôb in the Old Testament? Ten

- Exodus 12:22
- Leviticus 14:4, 14:6, 14:49, 14:51, 14:52

- Numbers 19:6, 19:18
- 1 Kings 4:33
- Psalm 51:7

Greek word: hýssōpos = hyssop

How many references are there hýssōpos to in the NT? Two
- John 19:29
- Hebrews 9:19

Historical Uses: The Israelites used hyssop when they sprinkled the blood of the Passover lamb on the lintels of their doors (Exodus 12:22). Hyssop was also used in purification rites (Leviticus 14:4, 6, 51, 52), sacrifices (Numbers 19:6), and was used to give Jesus sour wine when He was on the cross (John 19:29).

Modern Day Uses: Asthma, Bruises, Colic, Coughs and Cold, Digestive Problems, Insect Repellant, Menstrual Cramps, Poor Circulation, Urinary Tract Infections

Plant Properties: Antiviral, Expectorant, Stimulant

Modern Day Fun Fact: In the early 1990's researchers began to uncover the idea that the antiviral properties in hyssop could be effective in helping people who are HIV Positive.[33]

Since that time, numerous studies and clinical trials have been completed to test this hypothesis. According to this Canadian AIDS Treatment Information Exchange:

> "Test-tube studies show that hyssop stops the production of HIV without damaging the infected cells. These results have encouraged some people living with HIV to try the plant as an

antiviral. Anecdotal reports suggest that the plant is effective in treating HIV-related infections and increasing CD4+ cell counts."[34]

It will be interesting to watch these clinical trials go from in-vitro (test tube) trials to in-vivo (human) trials to see if the results found in the test tubes can translate and yield similar responses in the human body. If so, what a miraculous find.

Biblical History: It is impossible to identify the exact hyssop plant used in the Bible because the name *hyssop* was not given to a particular plant, but to a family of plants.

Biblical scholars agree that a variety of species from the hyssop family may have been used for different purposes at different times throughout biblical history. This is important because hyssop was used in so many different ways. The hyssop used in the Bible is probably one (or all) of the following three plants:

1. The common *hyssop* is a shrub with low, bushy stalks with numerous, small white flowers that are found in a bunch. Common *hyssop* would have been well suited to use as a brush to dab the blood of the Passover lambs on the lintels of homes of the Israelite families during Passover (Exodus 12:22).

2. Biblical hyssop could have also been the caper plant, or *Capparis spinosa* of Linnaeus. "It is a bright-green creeper, which climbs from the fissures of the rocks, is supposed to possess cleansing properties, and is capable of yielding a stick to which a sponge might be attached. It produces a fruit the size of a walnut, called the mountain pepper."[35]

3. Most scholars however are in favor of biblical hyssop being a type of marjoram (*Origanum maru*) and "having the fragrance of thyme, with a hot, pungent taste, and long slender stems."[36]

During the crucifixion of Jesus Christ, the soldiers are mentioned to have "filled a sponge with vinegar, and put it upon hyssop" (John 19:29). This is likely referring to a rod or reed of hyssop, which would have been about two feet long and tall enough to reach the mouth of Jesus on the cross.[37]

Chapter Fourteen

Myrrh

"All Your garments are fragrant with myrrh and aloes and cassia; out of ivory palaces stringed instruments have made You glad."

Psalm 45:8

In biblical times, myrrh is believed to have come from the *Balsamodendron myrrha* tree and is the gum, resin, or white liquid that flows from the bark when it has been cut. Myrrh exudes from the bark, or is obtained by incisions made in the bark, and appears in resinous, yellow drops, which gradually thicken and become harder. The smell is balsamic, and the taste bitter and slightly pungent.

Hebrew word: There are two Hebrew words for myrrh:

1. môr = an Arabian gum from the bark of a tree, used in sacred oil and in perfume
2. lôt = an aromatic gum exuded by the leaves of the rock rose

How many references are there to môr and lôt in the Old Testament? Fourteen

môr:
- Exodus 30:23
- Esther 2:12
- Psalm 45:8
- Proverbs 7:17
- Song of Solomon 1:13, 3:6, 4:6, 4:14, 5:1, 5:5, 5:13

lôt:
- Genesis 37:25, 43:11

Greek word: There are two Greek words for myrrh:

1. smurna = a bitter gum and costly perfume
2. smyrnízō = to mix and flavor with myrrh

How many references are there to smurna and smyrnízō in the NT? Three

smurna:
- Matthew 2:11
- John 19:39

smyrnízō:
- Mark 15:23

Historical Uses: Holy Anointing Oil (Exodus 30:23), Perfume (Esther 2:12, Psalm 45:8, Proverbs 7:17), Gift of the Magi (Matthew 2:11), Offered to Jesus on the cross to dull some of His pain (Mark 15:23), Embalming (John 19:39)

Modern Day Uses: Cough, Cuts and Wounds, Dermatitis, Diarrhea, Gum/Mouth Problems, Hemorrhoids, Indigestion, Skin Disorders, Stomach Ache, Yeast Infection

Plant Properties: Analgesic, Antibacterial, Antibiotic, Anti-fungal, Anti-inflammatory, Antiseptic, Astringent, Decongestant, Expectorant, Sedative

Modern Day Fun Fact: Myrrh is becoming one of the most popular oils to be studied among scientists and researchers.

In their 2001 study, entitled: *"Gift of the Magi" Bears Anti-Cancer Agents*, Mohamed M. Rafi, Ph.D. and Chi-Tang Ho, Ph.D. identified that:

> "The myrrh compound appears to kill cancer cells by inactivating a specific protein, called Bcl-2, which is overproduced by cancer cells, particularly in the breast and prostate."[38]

Of note, some types of Hodgkin's and Non-Hodgkin's Lymphoma (for instance, MALT, or Mucosa Associated Lymphoid Tissue) are also positive for the Bcl-2 protein. This is once again amazing news for me, as this is the type of cancer I have! The case study goes on to say that an:

> "...overproduction of this (Bcl-2) protein is believed to promote the growth of cancer cells and make cells more resistant to chemotherapy. As cancer is influenced by many mechanisms, the investigators are now in the process of trying to determine whether the compound also has other mechanisms of inhibitory action against cancer cells."[39]

This is just another way of how our modern day essential oils are so incredibly personal for me. I feel confident that when (remember, not *if*) my cancer returns, I can tap into the healing components of both frankincense and myrrh—my *sweet Jesus oils*.

The evidence-based research (that continues to grow) is proving to me that these oils can also help my body fight the cancer naturally, potentially reducing (if not altogether eliminating) the modern-day medicine I may also need.

Biblical History: In Mark 15:23 we find that Jesus was offered a "wine mingled with myrrh" which He did not take. Myrrh was often infused into wine to give it a more agreeable flavor and regularly offered to criminals just before their crucifixion.

The medicinal components of myrrh caused an anesthetic sensation to deaden some of the pain one would feel through the crucifixion and dying process (Proverbs 31:6). Traditionally, this wine and myrrh was:

> "...provided by an association of wealthy women in Jerusalem, who prepared it for (this) purpose."[40]

However, think back to what we revealed about aloes/sandalwood and the Jewish custom of burying someone. Just as it is unlikely that Jesus was given the same burial rites a Jew would normally have, I wondered if the people of Jerusalem would have spent the time, energy, and money to prepare this wine and myrrh for Jesus. My ponderings agreed with those of John Gill, who in his *Exposition of the Bible* suggests that the wine and myrrh given to Jesus Christ was more likely prepared by His friends Mary Magdalene, Martha, and "others."[41]

My brain has a difficult time grasping the greatness of Jesus' decision not to drink the wine and myrrh. Jesus had already been through so much; from sweating tears of blood in the Garden of Gethsemane, to His body being badly beaten and bruised. I would think any relief would be welcomed at that point. However, the torture would only continue on the cross, an intense pain He went into with full knowledge of exactly what it meant.

In his book, *A Doctor at Calvary*, Pierre Barbet beautifully describes the reality of the circumstances of the cross.

> "It will soon be three o'clock. At last! Jesus is holding out the whole time. Every now and then He draws Himself up. All His pains, His thirst, His cramps, the asphyxiation and the vibration of the two median nerves have not drawn one complaint from Him. But, while His friends are there indeed, His

Father, and this is the last ordeal, His Father seems to have forsaken Him. *Eli, Eli, lamma sabacthani?*

He now knows that He is going. He cries out *consummatum est*. The cup is drained, the work is complete. Then, drawing Himself up once more and as if to make us understand that He is dying of His own free will, *iterum clamans voce magna*: 'Father, into Thy hands I commend My Spirit' (*habens in potestate ponere animam suam*). He died when He willed to do so."[42]

The suffering, death, and resurrection of Jesus Christ is what separates Christianity from any other religion. And, when He was offered an option to dull some of His extreme pain, Jesus chose not to. He chose to take on the intense pressure and weight of every sin, every shame, every hurt, and every pain because He LOVES us.

God's love is so overwhelming, and way too much to grasp. We can only hold our hands in surrender as we humbly accept His love. There is no reason for us to hold on to God's love tightly out of fear that He will release His grip. He won't! And, while we will constantly fight the desire to work for our salvation, or fight the feelings of unworthiness for what Jesus Christ did for us, the cross tells us differently—it's already been done and we are worth everything!

Chapter Fifteen

Myrtle

"They found written in the law how the LORD had commanded through Moses that the sons of Israel should live in booths during the feast of the seventh month. So they proclaimed and circulated a proclamation in all their cities and in Jerusalem, saying, 'Go out to the hills, and bring olive branches and wild olive branches, myrtle branches, palm branches and branches of other leafy trees, to make booths, as it is written.'"

Nehemiah 8:14-15

Biblical myrtle was an evergreen tree, growing wild throughout the north of Africa, and parts of Asia. The leaves and branches were used to make medicine and temporary shelter for the Israelites during the festival of the seventh month as we find in Nehemiah 8:14-15.

Hebrew word: hădas = myrtle tree

How many references are there to hădas in the Old Testament? Six

- Nehemiah 8:15
- Isaiah 41:9, 55:13
- Zechariah 1:8, 1:10, 1:11

Greek word: myrtiá = myrtle

How many references are there to myrtiá in the NT? None

Historical Uses: Medicine and Temporary Shelter for the Israelites during the festival of the seventh month (Nehemiah 8:15)

Modern Day Uses: Bladder conditions, Bronchitis, Coughs and Colds, Diarrhea, Tuberculosis, Whooping Cough

Plant Properties: Antibacterial, Anti-inflammatory, Anti-Rheumatic, Anti-Viral, Astringent, Deodorant, Disinfectant, Expectorant, Sedative

Modern Day Fun Fact: *Myrtus communis* is proving to have high antibacterial and antimicrobial properties. In their *Evaluation of the Antimicrobial Properties of the Essential Oil of Myrtus communis*, researchers found the components of myrtle essential oil were effective against different strains of tuberculosis, even when modern-day pharmaceutical drugs were ineffective. Their findings showed that:

> "The essential oils screened in toto have a better antimicrobial activity than each single compound against all mycobacteria tested."[43]

Another section of this evaluation I found fascinating was that the researchers learned:

> "The chemical composition of the essential oil of *M. communis* exhibited qualitative differences that depended on different geographical areas and from the season in which the leaves were picked up."[44]

Before I began to use essential oils, I spent time researching the best oils to use. If I was going to start the journey of a more natural approach to healthcare for my entire family, I wanted to make sure our oils were pure and the absolute best products available. Again, if I was going to make this switch, I was going all-in.

During my research, I found information on different tests that can be done to test the purity and quality of each essential oil. These tests make sure there are no pesticides, herbicides, cross-contamination, or any synthetic materials when creating very high quality oils. I also found many chemistry composition charts with big fancy words that made absolutely no sense to me.

However, many articles also mentioned the importance of the geographical location of where the oils were sourced. This was honestly something I'd never considered before. The more I read, the more I understood how the geographical location, altitude, rain fall, amount of sunshine, temperature, and harvest seasons all have a great impact on the quality of the essential oil. There is something beautiful and pure about companies who source their oils from the very locations where God placed the plants to begin with.

Biblical History: The Hebrew name of Queen Esther in the Bible was Hadassah, which was derived from the Hebrew word *hădas*, meaning "myrtle".

> "He was bringing up Hadassah, that is Esther, his uncle's daughter, for she had no father or mother. Now the young lady was beautiful of form and face, and when her father and her mother died, Mordecai took her as his own daughter."
> *Esther 2:7*

With its dark green leaves, pretty white flowers, and dark berries, the myrtle tree is widely known for its fragrant and beautiful smell. Even to this day, the myrtle tree is still used regularly by the Jews in the Feast of Tabernacles (Nehemiah 8:14-15).[45] However, the potency of the sweet aroma can only be released after it has been bruised or crushed.

In a similar way, Esther was a woman filled with a tender heart and love for God and her people. Yet, her full potential was not released until after she endured some pretty intense trials and challenges.

She kept the secret about her Jewish heritage from her husband, the Persian King Xerxes (Esther 2:20), exposed Haman's plot to destroy the Jews, and ultimately stood up for her people to the King (Esther 7:1-6). Esther knew if she remained silent about Haman's plans, her family and friends could die. However, she also knew that if she spoke up, she could also be put to death, for she too was of Jewish heritage.

But instead of living in fear, Esther placed her trust in God, stood up for what she believed in, and did what was right even in the midst of facing death. What an incredible example to remember when we go through our own trials and difficult times.

Chapter Sixteen

Onycha

"Then the LORD said to Moses, 'Take for yourself spices, stacte and onycha and galbanum, spices with pure frankincense; there shall be an equal part of each. With it you shall make incense, a perfume, the work of a perfumer, salted, pure, and holy.'"

Exodus 30:34-35

Onycha is the most unusual and most controversial spice we will reveal in this study.

Hebrew word: shecheleth = nail or claw

How many references are there to shecheleth in the Old Testament? One

- Exodus 30:34

Greek word: onuz = nail or claw

How many references are there to onuz in the NT? None

Historical Uses: Holy Incense (Exodus 30:34)

Modern Day Fun Fact: Modern day onycha is most often distilled from the resin of the *Styrax benzoin* trees. This tree is believed to have originated in Laos and Vietnam, but now also grows in and around Malaysia, Java and Sumatra areas.

Styrax benzoin can reach 66ft in height and has leaves that are of oval shape with greenish-yellow flowers. Benzoin is extracted from the bark of the tree, which can continue to produce resin for fifteen to twenty years.[46]

Sometimes called the *Sumatra benzoin tree*, Sumatra benzoin is used in pharmaceutical preparations such as tincture benzoin (alcohol mixed with benzoin) because of its antimicrobial and antiseptic properties.

A different form of benzoin (Siam benzoin) is also used to flavor alcoholic and non-alcoholic beverages, baked goods, candy, dairy foods, gelatins, and puddings.[47]

Biblical History: There are four very different theories as to where biblical onycha came from.

1. The first theory is that biblical onycha was a spice derived from the closing flaps or the shell of a Red Sea mollusk (likely the genus *strombus*).[48,49] Many biblical scholars agree that the word *onycha* refers to the operculumor claw of one or more species of a shellfish. When burned the claw gave a sweet, yet musky odor.

   I found this to be both totally confusing and very intriguing at the same time. Onycha is only mentioned in Exodus 30:34, as an ingredient in the Holy Incense. Remember, this Holy Incense was meant to anoint the tent of meeting (tabernacle), was a pleasing aroma unto the Lord and though made by man, was for God alone—set apart and holy.

   While a majority of the biblical scholars agree on this theory, the confusion stems from an understanding that at this time in biblical history, *all* types of shellfish were an abomination. Anyone who even touched a shellfish to extract the onycha would be instantly unclean, this included the people God appointed to make the Holy Incense.

"Whatever in the water does not have fins and scales is abhorrent to you." *Leviticus 11:12*

2. The second theory, based largely on the abomination factor of a sea mollusk being used, is that onycha was really a mineral from the gemstone onyx. In the Septuagint, the original Greek word *onyx* also meant fingernail or animal claw.

In his research, *Onycha, Ingredient of the Ancient Jewish Incense: An Attempt to Identification*, Harold J. Abrahams shares that:

"...the nail or claw is actually an extended connotation of onyx, derived from the translucent and sometimes veined appearance of the gemstone onyx, its familiar meaning."

Abrahams goes on to say:

"It seems highly unlikely that the use of the mollusk or of parts of the mollusk was intended or permitted for rites in the Holy Tabernacle, and this is indeed confirmed by the famed theologian Nachmanides, who emphasized that the commandment concerning unclean animals pertained not only to dietary rules, but to the temple service as well."[50]

We find this precious stone adorning the breast-plate of the high priest and the shoulders of the ephod in Exodus 28:9-12, 20, 35:27; Job 28:16, and Ezekiel 28:13. We also find King David using onyx in 1 Chronicles 29:2 to provide for the house of God.

The confusion here is that onyx was used mostly for engraving and decoration purposes. Therefore it would seem unusual to use it as a fragrant odor, or for the purpose of the Holy Incense.

3. Some believe biblical onycha came from the *Styrax* species, perhaps either *S. tokinense* or *S. benzoin*, which would have been small shrubs or trees. The theory behind this idea is that especially *S. benzoin* had a vanilla-like scent. If added to the Holy Incense, it could give the incense a very pleasant scent.

   The argument to this theory is that these species of *Styrax* were not a native plant for the Israelites. *Styrax* grew in more Asian locations and would have needed to be traded, or exported.[51] Therefore, some believe it is unlikely that a spice, plant or oil would need to be imported in for use in the Holy Incense.[52]

4. The last theory is that biblical onycha was actually a type of cistus/rock rose species called *labdanum*. According to *All the Plants of the Bible* written by Winifred Walker, the rock rose is a bush that has been used in perfumes and incense for thousands of years and grows in Israel and Palestine.[53]

   This type of onycha is the most probable of the four theories and would make sense based on Abrahams understanding of biblical *labdanum*, where he writes:

   "The commercial article (*labdanum*) consists of dark-brown to blackish masses, with a gray fracture when fresh, or of cylindrical rolls, much like sticks of licorice, easily softened by the warmth of one's hand."[54]

Whichever theory you personally lean towards, may I give you two thoughts to consider?

1. The Holy Incense was for God alone and was pleasing to Him. In His infinite creativity, God created the mollusk, the gemstone, and the plants and was pleased with *everything* He created.

   "God saw all that He had made, and behold, it was very good. And there was evening and there was morning, the sixth day." *Genesis 1:31*

Nothing goes back to God that didn't first come from Him.

2. Not too long ago a friend asked me questions about the ingredients in this Holy Incense. She was thinking about making her own batch to know what it may have smelled like. However, she quickly changed her mind after reading Exodus 30:38:

   "Whoever shall make any like it (the Holy Incense), to use as perfume, shall be cut off from his people."

It is quite possible that only God, and the men He choose to make the Holy Incense in the Bible will ever know exactly what onycha was—and perhaps, that is not a bad thing!

Chapter Seventeen

Rose of Sharon

"I am the rose of Sharon, The lily of the valleys."

Song of Solomon 2:1

Biblical rose of Sharon was a flower from a fertile plain in the Holy Land named *Sharon*. This plain was known for its wines, flowers, and pastures. Sharon lies between the mountains of central Palestine and the Mediterranean Sea and north of the Joppa district on the east of the Jordan around Gilead and Bashan.

Hebrew word: There are two Hebrew words used to describe "Rose of Sharon":

1. chăbatstseleth = meadow-saffron, crocus, rose
2. Shârôn = a plain

How many references are there to chăbatstseleth in the Old Testament? Two

- Song of Solomon 2:1
- Isaiah 35:1

How many references are there to Shârôn in the Old Testament? Seven

- Joshua 12:18
- 1 Chronicles 5:16, 27:29
- Song of Solomon 2:1
- Isaiah 33:9, 35:2, 65:10

Greek word: There are two Greek words loosely related to chăbatstseleth, and one Greek word meaning Shârôn.

1. krinon = flower, lily, wildflower
2. anthos = a flower
3. Sárōn = plain or level, a level region extending from Caesarea of Palestine as far as Joppa, abounding in good pasture and famous for its fertility.

How many references are there to krinon in the New Testament? Two

- Matthew 6:28
- Luke 12:27

How many references are there to anthos in the New Testament? Three

- James 1:10, 11
- 1 Peter 1:24

How many references are there to Sárōn in the New Testament? One

- Acts 9:35

Modern Day Fun Fact: Though many people believe the rose of Sharon was a type of rose, the rose of Sharon from the Bible is more likely a type of crocus, or meadow saffron.

Some modern day scientists, researchers, and even some essential oil companies market the essential oils they study and produce from the rock rose (or cistus) as the same Rose of Sharon discussed in the Bible. However, the meadow saffron (Rose of Sharon from the Bible) and the cistus plant (modern day Rose of Sharon) are from two completely different plant families. The meadow saffron is classified as a plant in the *Colchicaceae family*,[55] whereas the rock rose plant comes from the *Cistaceae family*.[56]

Rose of Sharon from the Bible (Meadow Saffron) Scientific Classification:		Modern Day Rose of Sharon Cistus/Rock Rose Scientific Classification:	
Kingdom:	Plantae	Kingdom:	Plantae
(unranked):	Angiosperms	(unranked):	Angiosperms
(unranked):	Monocots	(unranked):	Eudicots
Order:	Liliales	(unranked):	Rosids
Family:	Colchicaceae	Order:	Malvales
Genus:	Colichicum	Family:	Cistaceae
Species:	*C. autumnale*	Genus:	*Cistus*

Biblical History: There is an interesting debate surrounding the rose of Sharon and whether or not this term may also be another Old Testament reference to Jesus Christ. While some biblical scholars disagree, many scholars believe when King Solomon says, *"I am the rose of Sharon, The lily of the valleys."* (Song of Solomon 2:1), this is really a reference about Jesus and His Church.

Considering the entire book of Song of Solomon is believed to be both about a love relationship between Solomon and his bride, and the love relationship between God and His bride (us), this correlation is quite possible.[57]

There are many parallels to consider, but these three stuck out the most to me:

1. The rose of Sharon was a flower that grew wild on the plain and was accessible to all people. In a similar way, the gift of Jesus Christ is free for anyone who chooses to believe in Him.

"For the wages of sin is death, but the gift of God is eternal life in Christ Jesus our Lord." *Romans 6:23*

2. Flowers that grow wild in a field are not planted by the hand of men, but are planted by God. While Jesus was born of Mary, He was not conceived by man, but rather conceived by the Holy Spirit. Think back to the study on myrtle and the scientific evidence of how the quality of plants will change if they are transplanted from their original geographical locations. Once again, I am reminded that there is beautiful purpose in God's design.

"Now the birth of Jesus Christ was as follows: when His mother Mary had been betrothed to Joseph, before they came together she was found to be with child by the Holy Spirit." *Matthew 1:18*

3. The fields where the rose of Sharon grew were known for their fertility and abundance. In the same way, Jesus told his disciples to share the message of His life, death, and resurrection in order to reach all people groups and grow the Kingdom of God.

"Then Jesus came up and spoke to them, saying, 'All authority has been given to Me in heaven and on earth. Go therefore and make disciples of all the nations, baptizing them in the name of the Father and the Son and the Holy Spirit, teaching them to observe all that I commanded you; and lo, I am with you always, even to the end of the age.'" *Matthew 28:18-20*

Chapter Eighteen

Spikenard

"Your shoots are an orchard of pomegranates with choice fruits, henna with nard plants, nard and saffron, calamus and cinnamon, with all the trees of frankincense, Myrrh and aloes, along with all the finest spices. You are a garden spring, a well of fresh water, and streams flowing from Lebanon."

Song of Solomon 4:13-15

Biblical spikenard or "nard" was the head or spike of an East Indian plant belonging to the genus *Valerianna*. Nard was not only a very expensive perfume whose oils were extracted in the preparation of a precious ointment, but according to the King James Dictionary, nard was also used for medicine.[58]

Hebrew word: nêrd = spikenard, nard, an odoriferous aromatic plant from India.

How many references are there to nêrd in the Old Testament? Three

- Song of Solomon 1:12, 4:13, 4:14

Greek word: nardos = head or spike which yields a juice of delicious odor when used (either pure or mixed) in the preparation of a most precious ointment, nard oil or ointment.

How many references are there to nardos in the NT? Two

- Mark 14:3
- John 12:3

Historical Uses: Medicine, Ointment, Perfume

Modern Day Fun Fact: There is a species of lavender that is often confused with spikenard. This lavender is called *Lavandula latifolia*, sometimes also called Spike Lavender. This plant is a small shrub closely related to true lavender (lavandula or lavandin).

It is also believed that in ancient Greece, this spike lavender was also called nard, not because of its relation or similarities to actual spikenard, but rather because this spike lavender came from the Syrian town of Naarda.[59]

With the names being so similar, spikenard and spike lavender, along with nard and nardos, one can justify where the confusion may have come from.

Biblical History: As we learned in *Chapter Six: Giving Jesus Your Best*, Biblical scholars believe the oil used by the woman who anointed Jesus and wiped His feet with her tears was pure liquid oil of spikenard:

> "...pure nard, unmixed and genuine; or liquid nard, which was drinkable, and easy to be poured out."[60]

While this account of the use of spikenard is the most popular story of spikenard in the Bible, I want to dive into the following passages in Song of Solomon.

> "How beautiful is your love, my sister, my bride! How much better is your love than wine, and the fragrance of your oils than all kinds of spices!"

"Your shoots are an orchard of pomegranates with choice fruits, henna with nard plants, nard and saffron, calamus and cinnamon, with all the trees of frankincense, myrrh and aloes, along with all the finest spices. You are a garden spring, a well of fresh water, and streams flowing from Lebanon." *Song of Solomon 4:10, 13-15*

Here we find spikenard mentioned along with many of the most valued and expensive aromatics. When read in its context we find that Solomon is describing his love and adoration for his bride, comparing her worth and value to the expensive and most valuable fragrances, oils, spices, and honey.

This verse does not infer that King Solomon actually married his sister, but rather these words are a parallel of Jesus Christ and His relationship to His church, as both His bride and His sister. The titles, names, and analogies used in chapter four of Song of Solomon are the expressions of Jesus' great love and adoration for His church (every true believer).

Just as people stand before God and their loved ones to enter into a marriage relationship, there is a marriage-covenant between Christ and His church. We find additional examples of this concept in Ephesians 5:22-32 where marriage is compared to Christ and the Church and also in all four New Testament Gospels, where Jesus is described as the Bridegroom.[61]

Just as Jesus is the Son of God the Father, when we choose to place our trust in Jesus Christ, we also become children of God the Father. We don't just become part of the family, we become His *sisters*, bought and paid for by the precious blood of the Bridegroom Himself.

Chapter Nineteen

Do You Know Jesus?

"For God so loved the world, that He gave His only begotten Son, that whoever believes in Him shall not perish, but have eternal life."

John 3:16

My relationship with Jesus Christ is *the* most important relationship in my life, more important than my husband and my children. When Jesus Christ died on the cross, He didn't just do so to check a box for His Father. He died on the cross out of an unconditional love and grace for me, and for *you*.

A couple of years ago, one of our pastors presented the following question: "Where would you be today if you weren't saved by God's love and grace?" WOW! To say I'd be a complete hot mess without God's love and grace would be an understatement.

It is by God's love and grace that I have not only survived cancer, but I have survived cancer three times. As I endured these trials, the display of God's love for me through the suffering of Jesus Christ gave me a different perspective of my own pain and suffering. If God was willing to allow Jesus to suffer and die for me, should I not be willing to live for Him – even through cancer?

It is by God's love and grace alone that I am not stuck in depression, or a whirlpool of destructive behaviors after the death of our daughter, our miscarriages, and three failed adoptions (seven children in total). We understand grief, pain, and sorrow. But, we also believe in a God:

> "...who did not spare His own Son, but delivered Him over for us all, how will He not also with Him freely give us all things?" *Romans 8:32*

It is by God's love and grace alone that I live in a time where emergency surgeries have literally saved my life twice. God could have chosen for me to be born in any country and in any time period. However, He chose for me to be born now, where I have been afforded the opportunity to continue living each day. I now see each day as a gift and understand the value of time. This allows me (and my husband) not to sweat the small stuff in life, but to live in gratitude of each day and moment we are given – knowing that in one breath all can be taken away.

It is by God's love and grace alone that I have learned how to keep my faith and trust in Him even when life around me felt like it was crumbling, and simply breathing was painful. He has never left me to deal with my problems alone, but has been a source of peace and comfort in even my darkest storms.

It is by God's love and grace alone that I am married to the most amazing man I've ever met, a man who loves me with an unconditional, selfless, patient, and adoring love. I could not imagine going through life with anyone else.

It is by God's love and grace alone that my soul has been redeemed, and my eternal future is secure.

> "For God so loved the world, that He gave His only begotten Son, that whoever believes in Him shall not perish, but have eternal life." *John 3:16*

As we wrap up this study my friends, I would be remiss if I did not share how you too can have a personal relationship with Jesus Christ and experience this same love and grace.

In a works-and-performance-based world, I know this seems too simple! But, the difficult part was done on the cross and now it is up to you to decide if you want to accept God's love for you. Come to Him just as you are. If you are sincere and willing to turn away from your sins, He will help you change what needs to be changed.

1. Admit you are a sinner and need Him.
2. Believe that Jesus Christ, God's son, died for you on the cross and rose from the dead.
3. Ask God to fill you with the Holy Spirit to guide your life.

There are no perfectly worded, magical prayers you have to say in order to become a believer of Jesus Christ. In fact, here is one of many prayers you could use:

> Dear God, I know I am imperfect. I am a sinner and ask that You would forgive me. I believe that your Son Jesus Christ died on the cross and rose from the dead. Please come into my life, as my Lord and Savior, filling me with your Holy Spirit. Show me the areas in my life that need to change, that I may serve and follow you. In Jesus's name, Amen.

That's it, friend!

If you chose to pray this prayer, WELCOME TO THE FAMILY!

To learn more about your new life decision, please share your decision with the men and women who love you most and go to my website: www.ericamcneal.com, where you can find some free resources to help you get started in your journey of faith.

Dig Deeper:
Reflection Questions

Chapter 1: Should Christians Use Essential Oils

1. What is the story of your first experience with essential oils?

2. Before learning about essential oils, where did you believe they came from?

3. In what ways have essential oils become distorted? How can we change this viewpoint?

4. How can essential oil companies improve the branding of the products they carry?

5. How have essential oils helped to aid your body?

Chapter 2: Just Keep Surfing

1. Where are you in your relationship with God?

A. Standing on the riverbank looking at the water = have not made a decision to follow Jesus?

B. Ankle-Deep = Have accepted Jesus Christ as your Lord and Savior?

C. On your Knees = Growing in your relationship with God through reading your Bible and prayer?

D. Wading in the water to your waist or loins = seeking God to help you navigate your decisions?

E. Swimming = total and complete faith in Jesus Christ and reliance on God to see you through the waves of life?

2. What can you do to become more consistent in your Bible reading and prayer life?

3. When the waves of life hit you, what is your first response? Is it to run away from God, or to run to God? What has shaped this response?

4. What is one life circumstance you are currently facing that would be easier if you went through it with God?

5. What tangible actions can you put into place that will take you to the next step of faith and help deepen your relationship with God?

Chapter 3: Our Rock and Healer

1. How has the phrase "God will not give you more than you can handle?" impacted your life?

2. What three actions can you take to share the love of God with your family or friends this week?

3. What does it mean that, "there is no retirement in our relationship with Jesus Christ?"

4. What are some of your personal life experiences that you can use to help heal the brokenness in someone else?

5. What weapon formed against you are you believing will prosper? Declare victory over that weapon in the name of Jesus Christ.

Chapter 4: Infused Oils Vs. Steam Distillation

1. Have you ever infused something? What did you do?

2. What do you think about the fact that slave women used to crush and grind the wheat and barley, but crushing plants and spices were given to men of high esteem?

3. How was Jesus "crushed for our iniquities" (Isaiah 53:5)?

4. Do you believe our sin is infused in the blood of Jesus Christ? Why or why not?

5. God didn't just allow Jesus to die for us. He allowed Jesus to suffer tremendously for us. Why do you think God allowed the suffering of Jesus to go so far?

Chapter 5: Old Testament Oil

1. What Bible verses are you aware of that are often taken out of context?

2. Has there ever been a Bible verse that you held onto, only to later realize the verse did not mean what you originally thought?

3. How can we understand the true intent of the Author when we read the Bible?

4. What resources do you currently use (or are available) to help you study the word of God?

5. What is one practical step you can take to dig deeper into the word of God and take your Bible study (and relationship) to the next level?

Chapter 6: Giving Jesus Your Best

1. What comes to mind as you think about the different words used for "love" in the conversation between Jesus and Peter found in John 21:15-17?

2. Has there ever been a time where God has asked if you "agape" Him, only to respond with "phileo"?

3. Why is the story of the woman who anointed the feet of Jesus found in Mark 14:3-9 so important?

4. What Christian boxes are you in the habit of checking off? How can you go from checking off the boxes to becoming more intentional in your walk with God?

5. How do you currently view all that you have or own? Is it God's? Is it solely yours? How can you use what God has loaned you to show His love for other people?

If you enjoyed these reflection questions, please go to www.ericamcneal.com for further study material on the oils and spices used in the Bible!

About the Author

Author of *Good Grief!* and *The Staycation Jar*, Erica McNeal has 18 years of experience in Youth, Marriage, and Women's Ministries. Erica is also a Health and Wellness Advocate with dōTERRA International.

A graduate of Hope International University, in Fullerton, CA, Erica received her B.A. in Church Ministry with an emphasis in Biblical Studies. She encourages and equips men and women by sharing her life experiences and her expertise of essential oils as a guest speaker.

Erica's hope is to be a resource as God uses her three battles with cancer and extensive child-loss to help men and women learn how to build stronger relationships, effectively love people who are hurting, and to advocate for health and wellness.

Erica's vision is to challenge the Christian line that states God will not give us more than we can handle because she believes that God will allow us to be stretched beyond our human capabilities in order to show us our need for Him, to deepen our faith, and to show us that HIS strength is limitless!

Contact Information
Website: www.ericamcneal.com
Twitter: @toddanderica

Other Books by
Erica McNeal

Good Grief! – In her debut work, Erica McNeal shares her story of cancer and child loss, and offers tangible solutions of *what not to say, what to say, and how to help* people in crisis and in grief.

She combats empty platitudes and Christian cliche's, giving her readers insight as to why certain words, actions, and inactions can hinder a grieving person's ability to move forward from their pain. *Good Grief!* can be found at LifeWay, Amazon, Barnes and Noble, and other online retailers.

Good Grief! Discussion Guide – Created for Grief Support, Women's, and Small Groups, Erica McNeal offers a six-week discussion guide (in a pdf format) for any church, person, or organization who wishes to dive deeper into *Good Grief!* While each session has unique qualities, the overall flow is: 1) Devotional, 2) Biblical Application, 3) Discussion Questions, and 4) Challenge of the Week. Each lesson is likely to take a group 45-60 minutes to discuss. Please go to www.ericamcneal.com for more information.

The Staycation Jar – This book was inspired by Todd and Erica McNeal's then six-year old daughter, who asked them to help her raise money for families with sick children. The storyline and all ideas came directly from one of their family staycations where they filled their days with creative meals, main events, silliness, and love projects.

The Staycation Jar gives over 200 family fun ideas of how to be intentional with your own family and is available exclusively on Amazon. All proceeds from the purchase of this book are donated to Faith Like A Child, Inc and over 35,000 copies have already been given away. This book is exclusively available on Amazon.

What Others Are Saying:

"The truth of God that has been experienced in the life of another is a foolproof guide. Erica McNeal has just this expertise from a life of perseverance in areas that may comfort us all."

—Tommy Nelson, Author and Pastor

"All of us will eventually have to walk through the valley either personally or with someone we love. *Good Grief!* will prepare you for that journey."

—Ken Davis, Author and Speaking Consultant

"If you are going through suffering, have gone through suffering, or know someone who is, then *Good Grief!* will be a tremendous guide and comfort for you."

—Sean McDowell, Author, Speaker, and Educator

"*Good Grief!* should be required reading for every pastor who wants to truly minister to the people of their church!"

—Kevin Baker, Pastor

"FANTASTIC! Erica McNeal speaks with the same candor and passion that can be found in her book *Good Grief!* She leaves the listener both inspired that someone so young has persevered through so much and feeling more equipped to love others through difficult times! The information she shares provides you with both tangible HELP & HOPE – a winning combination!!"

—Amber Robbins

"Erica has a knack for engaging her audience in a meaningful and powerful way. You feel as if you've known her all your life and want to hear more!"

—Rachel Baylor

"I can honestly say that *Good Grief!* changed the way in which I interact with others during their difficult times in life. I am always there to help others, but I've never known what to say. Now I do. Before reading this book, I would have felt awkward relaying my sympathies to others, especially if that person was clergy. But I'm very proud to say that this book has taken that fear away. It is a must read for all!"

—Melanie Jenkins, M.A.

"There is no better teacher than one who has learned through experience. In *Good Grief!*, Erica McNeal gives you and I a gift by openly sharing lessons learned in the midst of painful experiences. Lessons that will help us to better come alongside, and encourage those who grieve."

—Tom Dawson, Pastor,
US Air Force Chaplain

"Erica McNeal shares her journey with heartfelt passion. She shares not only from her experience, but connects with those who feel pain due to intense loss. Her godly wisdom will bring healing."

—Dr. Joseph C. Grana II,
Dean of Pacific Christian College
Ministry & Biblical Studies

References

1. "Aromatherapy and Essential Oils (PDQ®)." *National Cancer Institute.* Web. 21 Oct. 2014. <http://www.cancer.gov/cancertopics/pdq/cam/aromatherapy/healthprofessional>.

2. "Rose-Lynn Fisher /Topography of Tears." *Rose-Lynn Fisher /Topography of Tears.* Web. 30 Nov. 2014. <http://www.rose-lynnfisher.com/tears.html>.

3. "Open Letter to Christians Everywhere." *Erica McNeal.* 5 May 2014. Web. 30 Nov. 2014. <http://www.ericamcneal.com/christians/>.

4. You will find an almost exact vision by Jesus' disciple John in Revelation 22:2.

5. "Bible Commentaries : Over 90 Commentaries Freely Available." *StudyLight. org.* Web. 30 Nov. 2014. <http://www.studylight.org/commentaries/>.

6. McNeal, Erica. Good Grief: How to Create an Oasis When Life Is a Desert. 2011. Print.

7. "Oil - International Standard Bible Encyclopedia - Bible Encyclopedia - Study-Light.org." *StudyLight.org.* Web. 30 Nov. 2014. <http://www.studylight.org/encyclopedias/isb/view.cgi?number=6465>.

8. "Mill - Holman Bible Dictionary - Bible Dictionary - StudyLight.org." *Study-Light.org.* Web. 30 Nov. 2014. <http://www.studylight.org/dictionaries/hbd/view.cgi?n=4322>.

9. "Distillation Process." *dōTERRA.* dōTERRA International. Web. 30 Nov. 2014. <http://www.doterra.com/#/en/ourProducts/sourcing/process>.

10. Stewart, David. "THE BLOOD-BRAIN BARRIER." *THE BLOOD-BRAIN BARRIER.* Web. 30 Nov. 2014. <http://www.rnoel.50megs.com/pdf/theblood.htm>.

11. "Strong's Interlinear Bible Search - Proverbs 21:20." *StudyLight.org.* Web. 30 Nov. 2014. <http://www.studylight.org/desk/interlinear.cgi?search_form_type=interlinear&q1=Proverbs 21:20&ot=bhs&nt=wh&s=0&t3=str_nas&ns=0>.

12. John Gill's Exposition of the Bible, 1746-8

13. "Matthew Henry's Complete Commentary on the Bible." *StudyLight.org.* Web. 30 Nov. 2014. <http://www.studylight.org/commentaries/mhm/>.

14. "Frankincense - The King of Essential Oils - Dr. Hill." Vimeo. Web. 30 Nov. 2014. <http://*vimeo*.com/28065809>.

15. "Frankincense - The King of Essential Oils - Dr. Hill." *Vimeo*. Web. 30 Nov. 2014. <http://vimeo.com/28065809>.

16. Stewart, David. "THE BLOOD-BRAIN BARRIER." *THE BLOOD-BRAIN BARRIER*. Web. 30 Nov. 2014. <http://www.rnoel.50megs.com/pdf/theblood.htm>.

17. Thayer, Joseph Henry. The New Thayer's Greek-English Lexicon of the New Testament. Peabody, MA: Henderickson, 1981. Print.

18. "Burial - Hastings' Dictionary of the New Testament - Bible Dictionary - StudyLight.org." *StudyLight.org*. Web. 30 Nov. 2014. <http://www.studylight.org/dictionaries/hdn/view.cgi?n=388>.

19. Roy, Heli J. "Pennington Nutrition Series: Cinnamon." Pennington Biomedical Research Center. Web. 30 Nov. 2014. <http://www.pbrc.edu/training-and-education/pdf/pns/PNS_Cinnamon.pdf>.

20. Butler, Trent C., and Jody Waldrup. *Holman Bible Dictionary*. Nashville.: Holman Bible, 1991. Print.

21. Hay, IC, M. Jamieson, and AD Ormerod. "Randomized Trial of Aromatherapy. Successful Treatment for Alopecia Areata." *PubMed.gov*. U.S. National Library of Medicine, 1 Jan. 1998. Web. 30 Nov. 2014. <http://www.ncbi.nlm.nih.gov/pubmed/9828867>.

22. "Cedar - Hastings' Dictionary of the Bible - Bible Dictionary - StudyLight.org." *StudyLight.org*. Web. 30 Nov. 2014. <http://www.studylight.org/dictionaries/hdb/view.cgi?n=1221>.
    "Cedar - International Standard Bible Encyclopedia - Bible Encyclopedia - StudyLight.org." *StudyLight.org*. Web. 30 Nov. 2014. <http://www.studylight.org/encyclopedias/isb/view.cgi?number=1904>.

23. "Gopher - Easton's Bible Dictionary - Bible Dictionary - StudyLight.org." *StudyLight.org*. Web. 30 Nov. 2014. <http://www.studylight.org/dictionaries/ebd/view.cgi?n=1529>.

24. "Frankincense - Easton's Bible Dictionary – Bible Dictionary - StudyLight.org." *StudyLight.org*. Web. 11 Dec. 2014. <http://www.studylight.org/dictionaries/ebd/view.cgi?n=1382>.

25. "Frankincense - The King of Essential Oils - Dr. Hill." *Vimeo*. Web. 30 Nov. 2014. <http://vimeo.com/28065809>.

26. "Galbanum - King James Dictionary - Bible Dictionary - StudyLight.org." *StudyLight.org*. Web. 30 Nov. 2014. <http://www.studylight.org/dictionaries/kjd/view.cgi?n=2522>.

27. "Galbanum - Kitto's Popular Cyclopedia of Biblial Literature - Bible Encyclopedia - StudyLight.org." *StudyLight.org*. Web. 30 Nov. 2014. <http://www.studylight.org/encyclopedias/kbe/view.cgi?n=904>.

28. Grieve, M. A Modern Herbal; the Medicinal, Culinary, Cosmetic and Economic Properties, Cultivation and Folk-lore of Herbs, Grasses, Fungi, Shrubs, & Trees with All Their Modern Scientific Uses,. New York: Dover Publications, 1971. Print.

29. "Galbanum - Fausset's Bible Dictionary - Bible Dictionary - StudyLight.org." *StudyLight.org*. Web. 30 Nov. 2014. <http://www.studylight.org/dictionaries/fbd/view.cgi?n=1330>.

30. "Stacte - Easton's Bible Dictionary - Bible Dictionary - StudyLight.org." *StudyLight.org*. Web. 30 Nov. 2014. <http://www.studylight.org/dictionaries/ebd/view.cgi?n=3501>.

31. "Exodus Overview - Matthew Henry's Complete Commentary on the Bible." *StudyLight.org*. Web. 30 Nov. 2014. <http://www.studylight.org/commentaries/mhm/view.cgi?bk=ex&ch=30&vs=22>.

32. "Hyssop - Holman Bible Dictionary - Bible Dictionary - StudyLight.org." *StudyLight.org*. Web. 30 Nov. 2014. <http://www.studylight.org/dictionaries/hbd/view.cgi?n=2940>.

33. Kreis, W., MH Kaplan, J. Freeman, DK Sun, and PS Sarin. "Inhibition of HIV Replication by Hyssop Officinalis Extracts." *PubMed.gov*. U.S. National Library of Medicine. Web. 30 Nov. 2014. <http://www.ncbi.nlm.nih.gov/pubmed/1708226>.

34. "Herbal Therapies Used by People Living With HIV: Hyssop." *TheBody.com*. Web. 30 Nov. 2014. <http://www.thebody.com/content/art47500.html>.

35. "Hyssop – Fausset, Andrew R. – Fausset's Bible Dictionary - StudyLight.org." *StudyLight.org*. Web. 30 Nov. 2014. <http://www.studylight.org/dictionaries/fbd/view.cgi?n=1752>.

36. "Hyssop - Smith's Bible Dictionary - Bible Dictionary - StudyLight.org." *StudyLight.org*. Web. 30 Nov. 2014. <http://www.studylight.org/dictionaries/sbd/view.cgi?n=2075>.

37. "Hyssop - American Tract Society Bible Dictionary - Bible Dictionary - StudyLight.org." *StudyLight.org*. Web. 30 Nov. 2014. <http://www.studylight.org/dictionaries/ats/view.cgi?n=1035>.

38. American Chemical Society. "Gift Of The Magi" Bears Anti-Cancer Agents, Researchers Suggest." ScienceDaily. ScienceDaily, 5 December 2001. <www.sciencedaily.com/releases/2001/12/011205070038.htm>

39. American Chemical Society. "Gift Of The Magi" Bears Anti-Cancer Agents, Researchers Suggest." ScienceDaily. ScienceDaily, 5 December 2001. <www.sciencedaily.com/releases/2001/12/011205070038.htm>

40. Hanbury, Daniel, and Joseph Ince. "The Botanical Origin and Country of Myrrh." *Science Papers, Chiefly Pharmacological and Botanical.* London: Macmillan, 1876. 378-382. Print.

41. "Mark Overview - John Gill's Exposition on the Whole Bible." *StudyLight.org.* Web. 30 Nov. 2014. <http://www.studylight.org/commentaries/geb/view.cgi?bk= mr&ch=15&vs=23>.

42. Barbet, Pierre. A Doctor at Calvary; the Passion of Our Lord Jesus Christ as Described by a Surgeon,. New York: Kenedy, 1953. Print.

43. Zanetti, Stefania, Sara Cannas, Paola Molicotti, Alessandra Bua, Marina Cubeddu, Silvia Porcedda, Bruno Marongiu, and Leonardo Sechi. "Evaluation of the Antimicrobial Properties of the Essential Oil of Myrtus Communis L. against Clinical Strains of Mycobacterium Spp." *PubMed.gov.* U.S. National Library of Medicine, 29 July 2010. Web. 30 Nov. 2014.

44. Zanetti, Stefania, Sara Cannas, Paola Molicotti, Alessandra Bua, Marina Cubeddu, Silvia Porcedda, Bruno Marongiu, and Leonardo Sechi. "Evaluation of the Antimicrobial Properties of the Essential Oil of Myrtus Communis L. against Clinical Strains of Mycobacterium Spp." *PubMed.gov.* U.S. National Library of Medicine, 29 July 2010. Web. 30 Nov. 2014. <http://www.ncbi.nlm.nih.gov/pmc/articles/PMC2914267/>.

45. "Myrtle - Hastings' Dictionary of the Bible - Bible Dictionary - StudyLight.org." *StudyLight.org.* Web. 30 Nov. 2014. <http://www.studylight.org/dictionaries/hdb/view.cgi?n=3918>.

46. Ryman, Danièle. "Benzoin Essential Oil." *Aromatherapy Bible.* Web. 30 Nov. 2014. <http://aromatherapybible.com/benzoin/>.

47. "Benzoin Resin." *Wikipedia.* Wikimedia Foundation, 8 Apr. 2014. Web. 30 Nov. 2014. <http://en.wikipedia.org/wiki/Benzoin_resin>.

48. "Onycha - Holman Bible Dictionary - Bible Dictionary - StudyLight.org." *StudyLight.org.* Web. 30 Nov. 2014. <http://www.studylight.org/dictionaries/hbd/view.cgi?n=4720>.

49. "Onycha - Hastings' Dictionary of the Bible - Bible Dictionary - StudyLight.org." *StudyLight.org.* Web. 30 Nov. 2014. <http://www.studylight.org/dictionaries/hdb/view.cgi?n=4155>.

50. Abrahams, Harold J. "Onycha, Ingredient of the Ancient Jewish Incense: An Attempt at Identification." *Economic Botany* 33.2 (1979): 233-36. Print.

51. Ryman, Danièle. "Benzoin Essential Oil." *Aromatherapy Bible.* Web. 30 Nov. 2014. <http://aromatherapybible.com/benzoin/>.

52. Abrahams, Harold J. "Onycha, Ingredient of the Ancient Jewish Incense: An Attempt at Identification." *Economic Botany* 33.2 (1979): 233-36. Print.

53. Walker, Winifred. *All the Plants of the Bible*. New York: Harper, 1957. Print.

54. Abrahams, Harold J. "Onycha, Ingredient of the Ancient Jewish Incense: An Attempt at Identification." *Economic Botany* 33.2 (1979): 233-36. Print.

55. "Colchicaceae." *Wikipedia*. Wikimedia Foundation, 8 Oct. 2014. Web. 30 Nov. 2014. <http://en.wikipedia.org/wiki/Colchicaceae>.

56. "Cistaceae." *Wikipedia*. Wikimedia Foundation, 20 June 2014. Web. 30 Nov. 2014. <http://en.wikipedia.org/wiki/Cistaceae>.

57. "Song of Solomon Overview - Matthew Henry's Complete Commentary on the Bible." *StudyLight.org*. Web. 30 Nov. 2014. <http://www.studylight.org/commentaries/mhm/view.cgi?bk=so&ch=2&vs=1>.

58. "Nard - King James Dictionary - Bible Dictionary - StudyLight.org." *Study-Light.org*. Web. 30 Nov. 2014. <http://www.studylight.org/dictionaries/kjd/view.cgi?n=3750>.

59. Balchin, Maria. *Lavender the Genus Lavandula*. London: Taylor & Francis, 2002. Print.

60. "John Overview - John Gill's Exposition on the Whole Bible." *StudyLight.org*. Web. 30 Nov. 2014. <http://www.studylight.org/commentaries/geb/view.cgi?bk=42&ch=12&vs=3&search=spikenard>.

61. Matthew 9:15, Mark 2:19-20, Luke 5:34-35, John 3:29

Made in the USA
Lexington, KY
29 April 2017